LEONAR

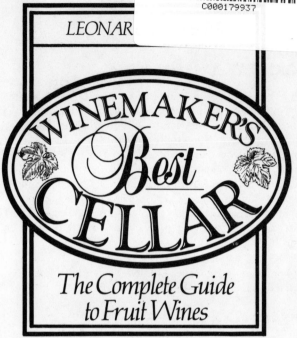

The Complete Guide to Fruit Wines

He causeth the grass to grow for the
cattle and herb for the service of
man: that he may bring forth food out
of the earth; and wine that maketh
glad the heart of man . . .

Psalm 104, verses 14, 15.

W. Foulsham & Co. Ltd.
London ● New York ● Toronto ● Cape Town
Sydney

ACKNOWLEDGEMENTS

My grateful thanks are extended to all those who assisted in some way in the preparation of this book. In particular, I have much appreciated the willing work of my friend, Janet Davidson and her daughter, Angela, who kindly undertook the marathon of typing my manuscripts. My thanks are also extended to my friend and colleague, Gwen Goodall, and to my daughter, Chris, who helped with the figures and line drawings. And lastly, a special thanks to my dear and long-suffering wife, Dora, whose kitchen equipment disappears for long periods and with monotonous regularity. The results are such, however, that her protestations are frequently only faintly heard!

W. Foulsham & Company Limited
Yeovil Road, Slough, Berkshire, SL1 4JH

ISBN 0– 572– 01394 –9

Copyright © 1987 Leonard Jones
Line drawings © 1987 W. Foulsham & Co. Ltd.

Printed in Great Britain at
St Edmundsbury Press Limited, Bury St Edmunds, Suffolk

Illustrations by Elaine Hill

CONTENTS

3

INTRODUCTION

Above all, *Winemaker's Best Cellar* seeks to put this ever-increasing and absorbing hobby into true perspective, so that the newcomer may avoid the pitfalls that many experience. It is quite irrational to outline how to make a gallon of wine to a beginner, using methods which tie up his limited equipment for sometimes months on end with, at best, the prospect of a very considerable failure rate. Yet far too many books appear to be written in this way. Whilst these marathons may ultimately bring success, they do quite frequently result in failure. No wonder so many become disillusioned at a very early stage. Authors quite naturally attempt to provide what beginners think they want, namely very little know-how and a plethora of recipes. But this is not the way to start. Consider the great variety of

wine types to be seen in any commercial wine store, and yet over 90% of these wines are produced from grapes alone.

Surely, all would-be amateur winemakers relish the prospect of its regular availability in the home. This book demonstrates how, with a minimum of effort and only modest expenditure, this can be easily achieved. Whether the reader intends to become an avid enthusiast, ultimately graduating to more scientific books, or merely wishes to go no further than making reasonable quantities of good wine without too much work, this is certainly the book with which to start. Only sufficient elementary technology to ensure success, with simple explanations, has been included.

In accordance with the above hypothesis, flower and vegetable wines have been excluded but, of course, this is not meant in any way to detract from the efficacy of wines so produced. In particular vegetable wines generally require considerably longer to mature and are therefore frustrating for a beginner. However, there is no real difficulty in producing these, and the reader should be able to tackle them with confidence, having mastered the techniques advocated here.

It is the deliberate intention not to overburden the reader with recipes, yet there are sufficient to enable a fair variety of wines to be built up. Having assimilated the information the reader will be well on the way to a satisfactory future performance and, with this in mind, the book includes a chapter on how to devise one's own recipes.

CHAPTER 1

A BRIEF HISTORY OF WINEMAKING TO DATE

Many books start by proclaiming that it is easy to make wine and indeed it is, for, given the right circumstances, it has virtually made itself, since the beginning of time!

In certain parts of the world, where temperatures and soil content are correct, some strains of grape have proved themselves to be the perfectly balanced fruit for fermentation. But as understanding has grown, it has been possible over the centuries for man to produce wines with increasing success from a variety of other ingredients.

Recorded history indicates that wine was first known to man around the Mediterranean possibly as far back as 10,000 B.C. When the skin of the ripe fruit breaks, the white 'bloom' that contains yeasts causes the sugar inside to ferment and produce alcohol. No doubt, in those far off days early man's first attempts to make alcohol resulted in wines which were very rough, of greatly varying quality and low in alcohol content, mainly because methods were crude and the action of yeasts was not fully understood or even recognized.

Wine became associated with magic and religion but despite this, in some areas, vineyards were planted and tended especially for the purpose of winemaking, and with the growth of the industry came the beginnings of innovation and elementary manufacturing techniques.

Wine is mentioned in very many places in the Bible and we are told not only of additions of spices and perfumes but of items of manufacturing equipment, such as fruit presses. Psalm 104 refers to 'Wine that maketh glad the heart of man'. But most common are warnings against drinking to excess, which is equally good advice today. Coming to the New Testament, the first recorded miracle was the turning of water into wine at the wedding feast in Cana of Galilee as recorded in St. John, chapter 2. And maybe there is a hint in this story of what has already been said regarding the varying quality of wines in those days, for we are told that the governor of the feast called the bridegroom and said to him 'Every man at the beginning doth set forth good wine and, when men have drunk well then that which is worse, but thou hast kept the good wine until now.'

Perhaps there is a suggestion, too, in this story of the low alcohol content of wines in those days, for we are told that six water pots of stone were used, each of two or three firkins apiece. This approximates to something in excess of 100 gallons, and that was merely to make up the deficit! From these·few references alone it is clear that wine was very much a part of life in the Middle East, and quite naturally wine and winemaking was to spread with Christendom and the Roman Empire throughout the whole of what is now referred to as the Western World.

Since the early part of the last century, there has been very considerable scientific advancement and, as in most other directions, this has brought about a gathering momentum of understanding and improvement. This has resulted in home winemaking being undertaken on a grander and certainly more successful scale than ever before, and is continually expanding at home and overseas.

The knowledge gained in recent years has provided tremendous scope and we are now able to make very pleasant and acceptable wines from dried, canned and frozen fruits all the year round, in addition to those from fresh fruits in season. Today, we are also helped cost-wise if we have ready access to the vast number of Pick-Your-Own fruit farms that have recently sprung up, and from these we can choose the very best and freshest fruits. Fruits can be stored in the freezer, making home winemakers independent of the seasons.

Lastly, we have available to us a goodly supply of fruits from the hedgerows just waiting to be picked. But such pickings should be avoided near busy trunk roads, both for safety reasons and the fact that the fruit will have been continually subjected to motor vehicle exhaust fumes. Both blackberries and elderberries are readily available in this way and make excellent wines, either alone or combined with other fruits.

The purpose of this book is to outline the way to good successful production levels, so that regular availability of wine in the home becomes a reality. Undoubtedly, fruit wines form the bulk of home production and will, I am sure, continue to do so. Generally speaking they make the best wines, create less difficulty, and mature more readily than the vegetable variety.

In this brief history of winemaking it is hoped the newcomer will learn sufficient to be assured of success. Certainly, if the recommendations advocated here are properly observed, it will be so. All that is required is a little expenditure and effort, combined with cleanliness and patience.

Nevertheless, even bearing in mind the advantages of our age, and having read this book, I feel bound to confess that it is unlikely wine will be made quite so readily, nor will it mature quite so quickly, as that produced at the far-off Galilean wedding feast nearly two thousand years ago!

CHAPTER 2

AN OUTLINE OF THE HOME WINEMAKING PROCESS

Very simply, wines are produced as follows:

(1)   (2)   (3)
Fruit+ Water + Sugar
Flavouring

<————————————— MUST —————————————>

Yeast Added
<————————————>
(Fermentation)

Transition
<————————>
Stage

(4)   (5)   (6)   (7)
Fruit   + Water + Ethyl   + Carbon
Flavouring   Alcohol   Dioxide

<———————————— WINE ————————————>

Chapter One mentioned the very beginnings of wine, and how grape wines nearly make themselves because grapes contain all of the items (1) (2) and (3) approximately in the correct proportions and the outer skins bear the yeast required to effect the transformation. In addition, they contain other essentials relating to the finished taste, such as tannin, acid, as well as further nutrients necessary to feed the yeast and thus support fermentation. These will be dealt with at greater length later.

It follows then, that whilst our own indigenous fruits may contain insufficient (or perhaps too much) of these essentials, good wines can be produced provided that we are able to make the necessary adjustments. These fruits, together with the excellent cultured yeasts now available, provide the basis of good home production.

It will be seen from the above 'equation' that items (1) and (2) and (4) and (5) are identical and as they appear on both sides of the fermentation equation, they cancel out and it is the sugar (3) which produces the ethyl alcohol (6). It also produces carbon dioxide (CO_2) (7), which is a colourless gas and plays no part in the finished wine. The gas is released to the atmosphere during fermentation through an airlock on top of the fermentation vessel. When we have made up items (1) (2) and (3) and balanced them correctly with the necessary additives in readiness for fermentation, it is referred to as the 'must'. When fermentation is complete it is wine.

The foregoing is an over-simplification and many other minor chemical reactions take place during fermentation and continuously throughout maturation, even though we are not aware of the changes that are occurring. The small chemical changes occurring during both of these stages vary from must to must to some extent and some are not yet fully understood, but we need not concern ourselves with them except to say that many of them are very important, indeed crucial, to creating a superb wine.

To start with, then, the must has to be prepared. There are numerous ways of doing this according to the wine style required; how we propose to achieve it and to some extent the quantity we wish to make.

Quantity is all-important. It is as easy to make five gallons in one batch as it is to make one gallon, and yet the beginner is quite understandably reluctant to attempt the larger batch for fear of failure. Authors are faced with the dilemma of wishing to advocate the former in the full knowledge that most beginners will be quite determined to prefer the latter. Too much emphasis either way can dampen enthusiasm. For this reason I have suggested methods which I am certain will result in success, irrespective of the amount that is made.

The best course of action is to start off in a small way with table wines, because these are the easiest to make and quickest to mature. Many of those made by using commercially prepared concentrates can be consumed after little or no maturation whatsoever. Then, afterwards, you may get busy on larger batches of country wines, including the table variety, for the longer term.

Another factor which causes beginners to opt for the smaller batch size is that they assume that they will be able to embark on a greater variety of styles. For this same reason they often choose a beginner's book which is simply laden with recipes for all manner of wines. Suffice it to say that it is highly unlikely the purchaser will ever make most of them, nor indeed is it necessary.

A few good recipes can be readily adapted to provide wines for most, if not all, domestic requirements thus enabling success not only for the enthusiast but also for the person wishing to start by making good wines in just the same way as he or she may produce an excellent Sunday lunch without necessarily claiming to be an expert caterer. Operating on a bulk basis, such a person may only require to replenish stocks by brewing two or three times a year. The work involved after fermentation is complete, similarly supports the view that bulk production is the better method.

When fermentation ceases one must not be discouraged to find the wine is rather unpalatable, to say the least, and that it may have a general appearance of cloudiness. To eliminate this cloudiness the wine is stabilized by 'racking' and sodium metabisulphite is added. Though this sounds rather scientific, racking merely means the operation of siphoning the wine off the yeast, pulp debris and deposited salts which have fallen to the bottom of the fermentation vessel. This combined deposit is known as the 'lees'. The first racking may not remove all the lees, as some yeast may still be active and remain in suspension a while longer. Sodium metabisulphite can either be added as a solution or in the form of readily available campden tablets, which are crushed and dissolved in the wine. This kills the remaining yeast, thus encouraging it to drop out of suspension in readiness for the next racking a while later.

Sometimes three or four rackings are necessary and even then the wine will not fall absolutely clear due to particles having insufficient size and/or gravity to fall out of suspension. In these cases it becomes necessary to resort to one of a number of fining techniques, filtering, or both. These operations, as all others, are dealt with fully in the appropriate later chapters.

When the wine has finally cleared it is then stored to mature in bulk. There are several reasons why it is better to mature in bulk initially, though final bottling is advocated as there are maturing advantages to be gained from both stages. Sometimes, even though a wine has been cleared, it can throw a sediment later — particularly red wines that are high in tannin — and following bulk storage this can, to a large extent, be removed before bottling.

When it is finally decided to bottle the wine, the sugar content is adjusted and the acid level checked according to the wine style and a final application of campden is made to reduce the possibility of re-fermentation.

Before leaving this chapter of outlining the process, something must be said about distillation. Roughly speaking, our finished wines range in alcohol content from approximately 10 to 17% by volume. Hence our wines contain in the order of 83 to 90% of water. Distillation is a means of increasing the percentage of ethyl alcohol by taking advantage of its lower boiling point to separate it from the water. However, the home winemaker must be warned that any attempt to do this can be highly dangerous. Ethyl alcohol, in the quantities present in our wines, is absolutely safe because it is inhibited by the large volume of water present, but more concentrated quantities of ethyl alcohol are highly flammable and, in vapour form, mixed with air, highly explosive.

Undoubtedly, the complication and expense necessary to obviate this danger are outside the scope of the home winemaker. Furthermore, any attempts to concentrate ethyl alcohol from our wines also concentrates methyl alcohol and other toxic substances. Too much absorbed into the system can cause blindness, brain damage and death.

For these reasons distillation is quite rightly illegal. The prospect should never be considered. Of course, the very small amounts of methyl alcohol in the wines advocated in this book and others, and also in commercial wines, is so dilute as to constitute no toxicity danger whatsoever.

CHAPTER 3

COMMERCIAL AND HOME-PRODUCED WINE STYLES

COMMERCIAL WINES

Commercially produced wines are available for all occasions in great variety, despite the fact that very nearly all of them are produced from grapes alone. They vary according to the variety of grape grown; the method of vinification adopted by the producer; they also vary according to their place of origin; the amount of sun available to the fruit and the nature of the ground in which the fruit is grown. Generally speaking, the more northerly disposed producers have to contend with rather more difficult weather conditions, but the table wines they produce are usually very refreshing, of a light nature and, being rather high in acid, can retain rather more residual sweetening sugar and still complement the accompanying food. Such wines are very popular today.

Nevertheless, there are many wines which are difficult to tell apart, particularly by the inexperienced majority, and the difficulty is made even greater because the produce, even from a given location, can vary very considerably from year to year due to climatic conditions. Everyone has heard of bad, good and vintage years.

Over the years it has been generally recognized that certain styles of wine are best suited to given occasions, but there should be no fixed rule about this and people should certainly be free to choose whatever style is preferred. It is generally agreed that the somewhat bolder reds rather tend to complement the stronger flavoured red meats, whilst lighter whites and rosés are better suited to white meats such as poultry and fish. These considerations are a useful guide to choice when a party sits down to a meal, and here the home winemaker should be better disposed than most in providing a variety of wines.

15

White wines can be produced by fermenting 'on the pulp' the juice of white grapes or, alternatively, by fermenting the juice only of either white or red grapes because the flesh of both is 'white'. It follows, then, that red wines are produced by fermenting red grapes 'on the pulp' thus including the skins which provide tannin and the richness of colour to the finished product. Removal of the pulp and pressing at an early stage during fermentation will produce a shade of rosé, but these shades can also be obtained by blending whites and reds together after fermentation. Today, blending is an accepted procedure amongst commercial winemakers, not only to adjust colour but mainly with a view to creating an overall balance from wines which, individually, are unbalanced. If done with understanding, correct marrying of such wines can produce superb wines from the mediocre. As this can also be of use to the home winemaker it is mentioned in greater detail in Chapter Nine.

The generally accepted wine styles and classifications are basically as follows:

Colour: White. Rosé. Red. Tawny.
Style: Table. Social. Dessert. Aperitif. Fortified.
Sweetness: Dry. Medium Dry. Medium. Sweet.

In the above table it will be noticed that tawny wines appear in addition to those already mentioned. These are mainly Sherries and certain Ports. In short, this colouring is the result of very slight oxidation during the maturation process. As wines in this category are fortified (that is to say their alcoholic strength is increased by the addition of expensive spirit), they are less likely to be made by the amateur. In the manufacturers' list of home wine kits both Sherry and Port styles are offered, but these are probably the most disappointing and unreal as their alcohol content is often 60% of that of the commercial product.

The alcohol content of the majority of table wines is in the order of 10 to 12%, although the slightly sweeter high acid white wines, so popular today, may only contain a mere 8%.

Social wines are regarded by some as something of an oddity because all wines are generally consumed on occasions which can be termed 'social'. Perhaps one could say this style is best drunk on long chatty evenings, when something rather more than a table wine is required without one becoming noticeably less 'social' as the evening wears on! Falling between table and dessert styles, social wines contain approximately 12 to 14% alcohol, and are medium in both body and sweetness.

Dessert wines are usually made to the limit of the yeast's alcohol tolerance containing some 16 to 17% alcohol; it is these that are sometimes fortified. However, due to the additional expense, most home winemakers do not do this, preferring to accept the maximum alcohol level obtainable by natural fermentation. To achieve this a process known as 'feeding' the sugar is adopted. In this way the yeast may be trained to accept a somewhat higher alcohol tolerance before exhaustion.

Aperitifs are another special type but they present no real difficulty. Even though high in alcohol they can be either sweet or dry. They are intended for consumption before a meal, generally in a small quantity, in order to stimulate the appetite. The name is derived from the Latin *aperire* (to open), and hence are a fitting opening to a meal.

HOME PRODUCTION

Today, the beginner may elect to make his first gallons from commercially produced concentrates. This will assure reasonable success and a product which will mature fairly quickly for early consumption. Such an approach is understandable enough, as a minimum of equipment is required and there are no real complications. All that is necessary is to extend the concentrate with sugar and water and add yeast.

Manufacturers have given the beginner much consideration, not only in simplifying procedure but also in recognizing his most important question — 'how soon?' Because of the public's impatience, they have developed some concentrates which are claimed to require virtually no maturation time whatsoever. Whilst these are acceptable for building up your cellar, it is nevertheless true that there is no real substitute for proper maturation over a period of time.

The majority of concentrates available run almost as a parallel to the true commercial wines they intend to simulate, such as red Bordeaux, Beaujolais, Chablis, but since 1981 a complication has arisen in identifying them, since EEC regulations have prevented concentrate manufacturers using such famous names. Most of the concentrates available are of the table variety, but others are also available, a number of which are a combination of grape and one of our more indigenous fruits. But our choice cannot match that available on the American Continent, where concentrates for just about everything can be purchased, including root crops.

17

Having made up a variety of concentrates for stock the amateur will quite naturally want to graduate towards his own wines, as these are even easier on the pocket and can produce some really superb results. The beginner should not be misled into thinking that these wines will be inferior to those produced from concentrates. Quite the reverse is true, and the feeling of satisfaction gained has engendered a life-long interest for many.

CHAPTER 4

SAFETY, HYGIENE AND PRESERVATION

In winemaking, cleanliness and hygiene are all-important, and as the manner of achieving these has a number of safety connotations, the word SAFETY also appears in the title of this chapter. It is perhaps well to record here that more accidents occur each year in the home than in industry, and they are often due to people undertaking unusual operations, using incorrect methods and make-shift equipment.

Apart from the obvious physical dangers to ourselves, sloppy methods and messy equipment can cause the product to go horribly wrong, and as winemaking is somewhat protracted, a considerable amount of time, effort and money can be expended before we actually find we have a problem. So we must consider the precautions which need to be taken and get used to their regular application as a matter of habit.

Some books, particularly older ones, have advocated sterilization of equipment by heating. Indeed, over the years, this has been a very common practice, particularly in laboratories where suitable facilities are available. It can be undertaken by subjecting equipment to steam heat or dry heating in ovens. But there are a number of disadvantages, especially in the home, as suitable steaming equipment is unlikely to be available and dry heating in an ordinary stove, even if large enough, has its own disadvantages. Quite apart from the unnecessary dangers to ourselves of scalding and burning, these methods have quite a high destruction rate, particularly when using equipment not specifically designed for this treatment. Furthermore, in a laboratory, should an item crack or shatter whilst being heated or cooled, a replacement is usually ready to hand. But for the home winemaker busy in mid-evening operations when all the shops are closed, such an occurrence could be catastrophic. Finally, the vast growth of plastics in recent years now means that many of our items of equipment are not suitable to withstand very high temperatures, though some may withstand boiling. An alternative method is required.

It is often said that there is nothing new in this world, and certainly this is true of our modern methods of sterilizing winemaking equipment. It has long been known that sulphur dioxide (SO_2) is a gas which spells death to bacterial infection, and way back in the Middle Ages the method of subjecting winemaking equipment to it for the purpose of 'sweetening' was well established. In those days this was done by the use of sulphur candles and matches which were lighted within, or in confined proximity to, the appropriate equipment. The sulphur burned with a characteristic unpleasant, pungent smell, greatly irritating to the respiratory system and producing a glutinous residue which could contaminate the equipment itself in other ways.

Sulphur dioxide is still used, but much more simply and effectively in the form of solutions made up from sodium metabisulphite. For years this has been available in powder or tablet form for home preservation of fruits and it is used extensively in the food industry as a preservative. For home winemakers, all that is necessary is to wash equipment thoroughly in detergent and rinse it clean, and then subject it to this sterilizing solution.

Both potassium and sodium metabisulphite can be used safely, but the latter has now become generally accepted by winemakers as it is somewhat stronger and considerably cheaper. It is cheaper to buy and easier to dissolve in powder form rather than as tablets, though the latter is often preferred by beginners, because they are convenient. Both forms are readily obtainable from all shops selling home wine products, including Boots, Woolworths and many other chain stores and supermarkets. The tablets are referred to as campden tablets.

For those preferring to use the powdered form, two stock solutions should be made up as follows:

a) <u>10% Stock Solution — 1 pint (570 ml)</u>

Dissolve 2 oz (57 g) sodium metabisulphite
in 1 pint (570 ml) warm water

This solution has reasonably good shelf life, but one pint (570 ml) should be sufficient for most winemakers. It should be renewed at six-monthly intervals. Quantities taken from this concentrated solution should not be put back for re-use as in the case of the 1% stock solution detailed below. One teaspoon (5 ml) is equivalent to one campden tablet and is therefore very convenient for adding to our finished wines in this measure. It must be kept in a well-stoppered bottle of plastic or glass and stored in a cool place.

b) <u>1% Stock Solution — $\frac{1}{2}$ gallon (2.25 litres)</u>

Dissolve $\frac{4}{5}$ oz (22.5 g) sodium metabisulphite
in $\frac{1}{2}$ gallon (2.25 litres) warm water

The shelf life of this solution is not so good as the 10% solution above and should be kept for no longer than two months. Being a weaker solution it is much more pleasant to work with, though for it to be of use the characteristic pungent smell of sulphur dioxide should be clearly apparent. If it is not, dispense with it. (Caution: those with asthmatic or bronchial conditions should avoid breathing the fumes, though).

Smaller items to be sterilized can be immersed in the solution; it can also be swilled around inside freshly washed vessels. A small quantity, say $\frac{1}{4}$ - $\frac{1}{2}$ inch (6 - 12 mm), should be swilled around and left in the bottom of all vessels, including closed buckets not in use and a cork, or preferably a rubber bung, fitted. If the bung is fitted with an airlock the solution should be added to that too. It must also be used in the airlock of vessels during fermentation. After a winemaking session the solution used at that time can be returned to the bulk for re-use if its potency has not been lost, but solution which has languished at the bottom of empty vessels in store should be thrown away when the vessels are brought into use.

The addition of citric acid to this solution to increase its effectiveness has been advocated in some books but this causes its sterilizing powers to be expended more quickly and in many instances this is not what is required. If necessary, I would prefer to use a stronger solution. If citric acid is added, the solution should be dispensed with once used.

The 1% solution can be made directly from the 10% stock solution merely by taking a measured quantity and adding to it nine measures of cold water. This obviously has advantages for the less prolific winemaker.

Half-gallon (2.25-litre) glass jars (winchesters) can often be obtained free from chemist shops. Needless to say, containers must be labelled and clearly marked with their contents, strength and the date the solution was prepared.

Beginners may prefer to use sodium metabisulphite in the form of campden tablets and indeed a stock of these is useful to every winemaker. Most recipe additions refer to sulphite in the form of campden tablets, so there can be no errors here. However, to make up just one pint (570 ml) of the weaker 1% solution, approximately 14 tablets are necessary, so even if you operate on a very small scale and opt for this method, buy plenty. Tubs and bottles containing the larger quantities work out very much cheaper. The tablets must always be crushed and dissolved in a little water before use.

Always have plenty of sodium metabisulphite around, in whichever form you prefer. Not only is it used for cleaning and wiping up spillages, but also in conjunction with newly prepared musts to prevent oxidation and the action of wild yeasts. It will also be seen, later in the book, that it is used in conjunction with post-fermentation and bottling operations. The mixed solutions are generally referred to as 'sulphite' and their use as 'sulphiting'.

Instead of employing sulphite for cleaning operations, you may use one of the excellent proprietory quick-acting cleaners and sterilizers, such as Chempro SDP. It is used by commercial breweries and is sold by most home wine suppliers. Such combined sterilizers and cleaners are excellent but one word of warning though, unlike sodium metabisulphite, they must NEVER be added to the wine process at ANY stage. They are chlorine-based and very corrosive and must be used and stored with care.

A final safety point since we have now begun to talk about chemicals and shall be referring to some others in succeeding chapters. The beginner should start by giving some thought to providing a place where these can be safely stored, out of reach of unsuspecting children and adults alike. If bottles and containers are used which have hitherto contained foodstuffs, the original labels *must* be removed and new labels firmly affixed stating clearly what is contained. Even so, they should not be left lying around.

SUMMING UP

1. Make up 10% and 1% stock sulphite solution as detailed.
2. Always keep a standby supply of campden tablets.
3. Remember, at least occasionally, to use Chempro SDP or a similar sterilant for all your equipment, including bottles and decanters, in order to remove stubborn stains and restore original glass sparkle.
4. Always clearly mark your stock sulphite and any other chemical solutions and add the date when made up. Change the date when renewed.
5. Always store your stock solutions and other chemicals away from the unsuspecting — especially children.
6. Do not keep either 1% or 10% stock solutions indefinitely. Renew as recommended.
7. Do not over-sulphite musts or finished wines.
8. Never add chlorine-based cleaners/sterilizers to wines — only sulphite.
9. Do not return 10% solution back to stock for re-use. If still potent, it can be diluted to a 1% solution with nine parts water for re-use as a cleaning agent.

CHAPTER 5

A REVIEW OF KITCHEN AND SPECIALIST EQUIPMENT

Expense and disappointment may be avoided if suitable equipment is obtained and used from the start. The advantages of bulk production have already been discussed, the only major difference being the cost of larger vessels, which is not excessive. Nevertheless, there is no need to be too concerned about the additional cost of changing later, as one or two vessels of smaller size are always useful when scale is increased. One-gallon (5-litre) demijohns are in fact the ideal size for maturation after fermentation is complete.

The minimum equipment is that offered in kit form by proprietary concentrate manufacturers and equipment suppliers: with anything less, wine could not possibly be made. Most kits never advocate enough equipment. Manufacturers obviously have a desire to attract the greatest number to winemaking by offering kits at an absolutely minimal price, but bearing in mind the high potential failure rate, they may well be doing themselves and home winemaking a grave injustice. I know of a number of people who say they have used such kits but are now no longer interested because 'things didn't seem to work out'.

Whilst such people were obviously beginners, they were nevertheless making up musts from concentrates produced by experts and which therefore were presumably balanced in every detail and I am quite certain that the root causes of their problems were a lack of basic fermentation knowledge and incorrect (usually too low) temperature. These two factors are inter-related and are dealt with in Chapter Seven on fermentation. Many of these kits are purchased at Christmas time as gifts, with the result that many an unsuspecting novice sets forth to make his first gallon during January and February — the two coldest months of the year. During summer such kits would no doubt ferment well, without any special attention, but not in the winter. Temperature is a very important factor which must be controlled if the yeast is to function correctly. Yet, though control is reasonably simple often its importance is not stressed sufficiently. The matter of correct temperature during fermentation and the equipment required to supply it, is so important that a full chapter is given over to the subject.

At this point the novice should take heart. What has been said on this subject is not intended to be offputting or to make life difficult or expensive; quite the reverse. Like all applications of elementary science it is intended to make winemaking easier whilst assuring a very high rate of success.

From a study of equipment from the basic stage through to comprehensive production in both scale and variety, it will be appreciated that wine from commercial concentrates requires the least apparatus. In fact, many of the items can be found as part of everyday kitchen equipment. However, the newcomer will probably soon become sufficiently enthusiastic as to want to operate on a wider horizon; it is a fascinating prospect and any money spent on equipment will be saved many times over, not only in reduced outlay for ingredients, but in creating vastly superior products and going a long way to eliminate failure.

USEFUL STANDARD KITCHEN ITEMS

Large saucepan

Preferably of approximately one gallon (5 litre) or more capacity. This should be of aluminium or stainless steel, but avoid the more expensive type with copper bottoms — copper, brass and iron are dissolved by wine acids, creating difficult hazes in the finished wine and unsavoury flavours, and the resultant wines may be toxic! Enamelled saucepans may be used providing that they are not chipped.

Long-handled spoon

This is used for stirring to dissolve sugar and for turning in the fruit during pulp fermentation. In the kitchen these are often of wood, which is acceptable. Alternatively, a very long-handled plastic spoon can be obtained cheaply from home winemaking suppliers and cookshops.

Kitchen scales

Preferably of the beam type with weights, as these are generally more accurate and may also be suitable for measuring small quantities of additives, but the latter can be better dealt with separately as described later.

Useful Standard Kitchen Items

Nylon sieve

Some sieves for kitchen use are of stainless steel, but where liquids are strained great care should be exercised to ensure that *all* parts are stainless steel. Nylon sieves are cheap, readily obtainable and equally effective.

Measuring jug

Minimum 1 pint (570 ml) capacity. These are universally available in all kitchens, they may be of either heat resistant glass or plastic.

Citrus fruit squeezer

Both glass or plastic are equally suitable. If buying a new one ensure that the dome is of sufficient size. Some are so tiny that only the smallest oranges and lemons can be satisfactorily squeezed.

Universal kitchen mincer

Often used by winemakers, especially to reduce raisins or sultanas for addition to a must.

Potato peeler

Keep a well-sharpened one handy to peel the outer skins of oranges or lemons in much the same way as peeling potatoes. These outer slivers of peel are often added to a must.

Kitchen kettle

As this is only used for heating water, a kitchen kettle in any material is suitable.

BASIC WINEMAKING EQUIPMENT

1-gallon (5-litre) demijohns

When making 1-gallon (5-litre) batches this is the essential vessel and demijohns are also often used for bulk storage prior to bottling. Accordingly, they can be obtained either in clear glass or tinted dark brown, the latter protecting the colour of red and rosé wines from sunlight during long-term storage. Clear demijohns allow you to observe the fermentation process and are also suitable for the storage of white wines. Both have advantages; but if only one demijohn is being purchased, then perhaps it is better to buy a tinted one, as is normally supplied with basic winemaking kits.

Care should be taken to acquire winemaking demijohns rather than the similar product used for the sale of cider. The latter are slightly smaller, including the opening and can easily be identified by the thread in the glass at the neck for fitting the commercially applied screw cap. Of course, a supply of this type at the right price for storage purposes should not be refused! Winemaking demijohns are readily obtainable from all homebrew suppliers.

Bored rubber bung and plain cork

These can be purchased from the same source as the demijohns, but care should be taken to ensure that the bungs obtained fit the neck of the demijohn purchased. The bung is bored to receive a fermentation airlock, which should always be used for this purpose. A demijohn cork and not a rubber bung must, however, be used for bulk storage. Rubber bungs exclude air and are therefore not suitable for maturing wine and, over a period, tend to seize in the vessel neck.

Glass syphon tube

This syphon tube has its lower end turned up so that when syphoning newly fermented wine from the lees, wine is drawn from above rather than below the tube, thus drawing clear wine and leaving the bulk of the lees behind for disposal. A weakness of this item is that when the manufacturer heats the glass to form the curve, the glass is stretched very thin and is therefore fragile on the outer radius, so that it is very easy to break the glass tube if it is roughly dropped to the bottom of the vessel. An alternative to the glass syphon tube is one of plastic, with a specially designed fitment at the lower end, which is virtually indestructible.

Plastic tubing

This is used in conjunction with the syphon tube above, and a 6 ft (2 metre) length is recommended so as to provide a good length of fall when required. A good fall is particularly useful when used in conjunction with a filter unit. Rubber tubing should not be used as it may impart a taste to the wine.

Fermentation airlocks

There are many patterns of these available and the actual type used is purely a matter of choice since they all perform equally well. They are used with a quantity of sulphite added to their bubbling chamber, so as to allow continuous escape of the carbon dioxide gas created by fermentation whilst preventing air from entering the vessel. Some are made from glass tube. Unfortunately these are very fragile and vulnerable, and are easily broken if knocked. I prefer the clear plastic type illustrated: they are cheap, easy to use and give a ready indication of the rate of fermentation. For 5-gallon (23-litre) batches a larger version is obtainable.

Basic Winemaking Equipment (for 1-gallon (5-litre) batches)

Plastic bucket

Plastic buckets are very cheap, particularly those produced in a variety of colours for general household use. However, these are not really suitable for winemaking, particularly the yellow ones which may contain cadmium. Though a little more expensive, plastic winemaking buckets made from food grade plastic are now produced in a variety of sizes. It is better to purchase these and retain them for winemaking only rather than to press into service a standard household bucket which has been, or is likely to be, used for domestic cleaning purposes.

Winemaking buckets are invariably of white high density polyethylene or PVC and being a relatively hard, smooth plastic they keep their shape well and are easy to keep clean. They also have a close-fitting snap-on lid specifically designed for winemaking. Such buckets are used for primary fermentation when fermenting on the pulp, and since this stage requires a large volume of air, the bucket should be of somewhat larger capacity than the batch of wine being produced. For 1-gallon (5-litre) batches a 2-gallon (10-litre) bucket is recommended. Such a bucket can also be used as a vessel into which to rack newly fermented wine.

Plastic funnel

This should be of the same material as the bucket. The largest funnel available, which has a stem that will fit into the neck of the demijohn, should be obtained. The funnel stem often has a few moulded ribs on the outer surface at the junction of tube and cone so as to maintain a space for the escape of air from the vessel when the funnel is in use.

Straining cloth or bag

These are usually of nylon and are available in coarse and fine grades. The coarse grade is quite suitable for general use. A cloth will be needed for use with the funnel; for the bucket, a bag is better. Both can be held in position during straining by three or four of the spring type of clothes peg.

Wine bottles

More will be said of these in the bottling section, but for the sake of professionalism, please, only use proper wine bottles! Bottles with a hollowed 'punt' in the bottom are best and 1 gallon of wine (5 litres) will fill six of these, leaving a little for tasting as a promise of things to come! White wines can be put into clear or coloured bottles, but red wines must be stored in coloured bottles only.

Corks

The corks illustrated on page 29 are of the flanged type often used commercially for Sherry etc. and are not strictly correct for straight, unfortified wines. However, as this start to winemaking employs only basic equipment and no cork fitting tool is advocated, this type of cork is much simpler to fit. They are readily available from all suppliers. Of course, once a bottle is emptied, corks must not be re-used due to the possibility of contamination.

Thermometer

The importance of temperature in fermentation has already been stressed and therefore, a thermometer is essential. A good, clearly read thermometer should be obtained, having a scale slightly exceeding 212°F (100°C) so that it will have the maximum range of uses. Although temperature is very important, expensive thermometers with clinical accuracy are not necessary.

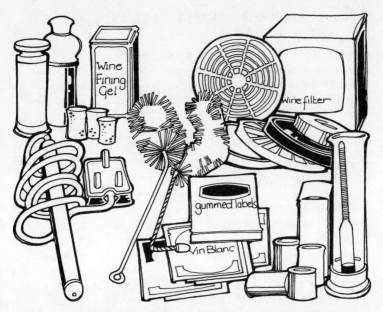

Recommended Additional Equipment (for 1-gallon (5-litre) batches)

This then is the basic equipment for all winemaking, and under favourable conditions it is possible to produce good wine simply using these pieces of equipment. They do not, however, take into account the very real possibility of there being too low a temperature and, of course, they assume that the wine will fall clear of its own accord. There is no way of measuring the original and final sugar content so it is impossible to assess the final alcohol content available, and no provision is made for a professional presentation of the finished product.

Nevertheless the total cost of all the equipment, plus a commercial concentrate and sugar to make six bottles of wine, will cost less than four bottles of a similar commercially produced wine at supermarket prices. And the equipment is available for continued future use. The next six bottles from a concentrate can be made for little more than the price of one commercial equivalent and using some of the recipes in this book, the outlay can be even less.

Viewed in this way the beginner may decide to purchase some, if not all, of the more advanced items listed below and so gain control of a really satisfactory fermentation whilst also greatly improving the finished quality and presentation.

RECOMMENDED ADDITIONAL EQUIPMENT

Electric heater

There are a number of electric heaters on the market and to some extent the pattern of one's production tends to dictate which type should be used, though there are one or two forms available which, in my own opinion, should be avoided.

Some type of heating is generally necessary, even though at times this may only be a slight need. A full discussion of the suitability of the various types of heaters are dealt with under the subject of fermentation (Chapter 7).

Hydrometer

This is a virtually indispensable piece of apparatus for any wine-maker, particularly when making wines other than from concentrates, and when formulating one's own recipes as outlined in Chapter 14. It enables the winemaker to assess the initial and final sugar content and hence determine the alcohol content; it is also useful when sweetening finished wines.

Very accurate types, as used in laboratories for measuring the specific gravity of liquids for experimental purposes, are expensive and usually two or more are necessary because of their limited range. The far cheaper, but slightly less accurate hydrometers designed especially for home winemaking are ideal for our purpose. These operate on exactly the same principle and generally include very convenient scales of alcohol and sugar content.

Trial jar

This is a simple, straight-sided jar of convenient size and shape in which to float a hydrometer when measuring the gravity of a must or finished wine. A separate plastic base is available for the cheaper variety, as illustrated, but the more expensive ones have a similarly shaped integral glass base.

Filter unit

In addition to fining agents, a filter eventually finds its way into the possession of all serious winemakers. Some deplore the use of a filter, though I find it difficult to accept their reasons; commercial winemakers invariably use filters. The range available to the home winemaker is dealt with in Chapter Eight.

Demijohn brush

This is a wire-based nylon brush and is shaped, or can be shaped, so as to be able to clean a demijohn interior thoroughly, including under the shoulder. Unless one is prepared to use a powerful cleaning compound such as Chempro SDP regularly, such a brush, used with a good detergent, will be necessary to remove stubborn stains etc. from the inside of these vessels.

Bottle brush

The use of this is straightforward and should be applied with a good detergent solution to each and every wine bottle before filling operations begin. The brush is usually straight and is designed to clean the punted bases of certain bottles.

Straight-sided corks

These are standard wine bottle corks and are available from all homebrew suppliers. Unfortunately, they have become extremely expensive in recent years. Good quality corks are, however, very necessary to the home winemaker, especially for long term maturing and they must never be salvaged for 'a second time around'.

Cork-fitting tools

The use of a specially designed tool is advised to fit wine corks. There are a number of versions available, ranging from the small, inexpensive types illustrated, through to large vertical versions best described as machines.

Bottle caps

These are fitted over the bottle neck after the cork has been inserted. They give the finished bottling a professional look and, whilst allowing the cork to breathe, they prevent it from drying out in storage. A number of types and colours are available and their use helps to aid recognition.

Labels

Some form of labelling must be used, and it should be attractive if possible. At worst, some form of gummed label can be used, so as to identify the bottle contents at a later date. These matters are dealt with at greater length in Chapter Nine.

It is difficult, in these times of inflation, to specify the cost of equipment, as any figure quoted very soon becomes out of date. Therefore, in an effort to make costs meaningful I feel it best to relate any expenditure on equipment to the cost of commercially produced wines as the price of these is likely to rise in similar proportion. These latter items of recommended additional equipment should cost in total no more than eight bottles of commercially produced table wine at supermarket prices.

Having in mind, then, the cost of the items in both of these sections, successful production and presentation of six bottles of good quality wine can be undertaken for a total outlay of no more than a dozen supermarket bottles, thenceforth each bottle produced will cost about one sixth of supermarket prices! On this basis it is anticipated that few, if any, would consider such an outlay to be excessive.

But be warned: at these prices your stocks will not last nearly so long!

A RANGE OF CHEMICALS AND CHEMICAL TESTING EQUIPMENT

As you progress, particularly when contemplating operations on a larger scale, you will naturally seek to employ those features which clearly distinguish the superb from the poor. In fact, some years ago a colleague, when sampling my wines, suggested to me that home wines always seemed to fall into one of these two categories. I hasten to add that I made no attempt to enquire into which category he placed mine!

The difference lies, to a large extent, in the judicious use of the chemical additives listed below by someone who knows what he is doing rather than someone who merely hopes for the best.

At first sight the list may appear to be rather forbidding but it is not. All of the materials are available at very low cost and in fact the most expensive, the wine titration kit for checking the acid levels, is as cheap as it is simple to use. It can be obtained for about half the cost of a bottle of good, commercial table wine.

The way to start is to purchase only those items immediately required and then to go on to replace expended stock.

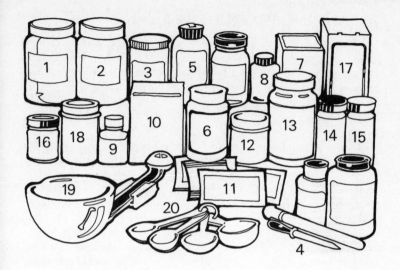

Useful Chemicals and Chemical Equipment

1. Citric Acid ⎫
2. Tartaric Acid ⎬ The three fruit acids used by wine-
3. Malic Acid ⎭ makers

4. Wine titration kit — To measure acid in a must or wine

5. Liquid wine tannin ⎫ Provides astringency to the taste of
6. Powdered wine tannin ⎭ a wine

7. Yeast nutrient tablets ⎫
8. Nutrient ⎬ Additives to feed yeast and create a
9. Vitamin B₁ tablets ⎭ vigorous and sustained fermentation

10. Pectolytic enzyme — To break down haze-forming pectin in a must

11. Yeast (packets) — Without which wine cannot be made

12. Campden tablets ⎫ To inhibit fermentation in a fin-
13. Sodium metabisulphite ⎭ ished wine and also a sterilized agent throughout

14. Potassium sorbate — An extremely good inhibitor of fermentation

15. Precipitated chalk — To reduce acidity in a wine when necessary (see also page 97)

16. Amylase — To break down haze-forming starch in a must

17. Wine fining gel ⎫ To clear colloidal hazes from fin-
18. Bentonite ⎭ ished wines

19. Dr Oetker balance — For weighing small quantities

20. Set of standard measuring spoons — To ensure volumetric accuracy

EXPANDING PRODUCTION

In the foregoing sections of this chapter, all the basic and rec-ommended items of equipment have been covered, together with the chemicals etc. for good home production in 1-gallon (5-litre) batches. It has also been demonstrated just how cheaply these can be obtained. It will now be seen just how easy and inexpensive it is to start making wine in 5-gallon (23-litre) batches and hence reap the greater benefits.

To the uninitiated, 5 gallons (23 litres) of wine sounds an awful lot and to refer to it as representing some 32 bottles only seems to cause them to view such a prolific output with even more incredulity and to conclude that those who have graduated to this level of production must be fast acquiring a drink problem! Yet 32 bottles is only sufficient for a supply of one bottle per week per household for a period of about seven months. Certainly no average family of four is ever going to be in danger of drunkenness from imbibing at this level. In fact, if wines are matured for an average period of one year, it is necessary to double the above amount for stock. Two bottles can very easily be consumed on a Sunday, one over lunch and another socially in the evening. Even at these modest levels it can be easily assessed that a stock of some 150–200 bottles is not unduly high. Every winemaker must assess individual household require-ments for himself but certainly, viewed in this way, the disadvan-tages of 1-gallon (5-litre) batches become clear. And not only are the larger batches easier to make, but they mean that the busy business man or woman need only brew a few times each year to meet the levels of stock outlined above.

So why not 10-, 15- or 20-gallon (46-75-or 90-litre) batches? So far as fermentation is concerned they will ferment as readily, if not more readily, than 5-gallon (23-litre) batches. But preparing the must for 10 gallons (46 litres) is, perhaps, as large a domestic undertaking as one would wish to countenance at any one time and, of course, 10 gallons (46 litres) of wine plus its container weighs something over one hundredweight (50 kg), which, at times, needs to be lifted to table height at least. A 5-gallon (23-litre) fermenter in its container can be lifted readily by a healthy adult on to a table, and maybe two adults would have no difficulty in lifting 10 gallons (46 litres), but anything larger is likely to cause problems.

10-gallon (46-litre) fermenter

A variety of such containers can be obtained, including glass carboys similar to those shown on page 38. In my view, the use of plastic for winemaking vessels is something of a problem. When full, plastic fermenters tend to distort if lifted, even though a handle is usually moulded into them for this purpose. This can cause problems at the airlock, when sulphite solution may be drawn into the fermenting must or, more often, the solution is blown out by air or liquid exhausting through the airlock. The fermenter illustrated does not suffer in this way as it can be moved around by handling the substantial cage in which it is cradled.

Where plastic is preferred, only purchase new containers sold for the purpose. I once acquired a 5-gallon (23-litre) container that was identical to containers being sold by homebrew shops at that time, but unfortunately it had previously contained a disinfectant and 5 gallons (23 litres) of Sauternes were completely ruined. A very expensive container indeed! Of course, I knew it had been used for other purposes before I acquired it, but unfortunately persistent washing and bleaching, including a spell of about 12 months in the yard minus its cap was not enough. In fact the molecular structure of these plastics is such as to trap traces of liquids in thousands of tiny pockets, which invariably escape at a later date. A vigorous fermentation with all its attendant bubbling and gassing will certainly release them!

For very similar reasons, plastic is unsuitable for longer term storage purposes; never store finished wine in a plastic container for more than a few weeks at most. Undoubtedly, glass is best for winemaking vessels. Fermentation can be readily observed and before use they can be seen to be clean.

This fermenter is shown rigged (page 38) with an airlock and heater unit, ready for the fermentation process.

5-gallon (23-litre) carboy

These are perhaps the best vessels for home fermenting and storage. They are readily obtainable from most suppliers and are relatively inexpensive. They come supplied in the cradle as shown (page 38) and are available in both clear and green-tinted glass. Such a carboy will cost about the same as five 1-gallon (5-litre) demijohns. If the carboy is to be used exclusively for fermenting then the clear glass is easier to see through, but if the vessel is to be employed for maturing, then a green one would be better. Otherwise it may be necessary to cover the vessel when red wines and rosé are stored. These factors are similar to those applying to bottles, which have already been discussed. This fermenter is shown with an airlock and thermostatically controlled heater unit fitted (page 38).

5$\frac{1}{2}$-gallon (25-litre) fermenter

This is very similar to the carboy mentioned above and is similarly priced. Though of better quality, it is, however, necessary to provide a container for it. Unless you have the timber available, the $\frac{1}{2}$ in (12mm) plywood for the case illustrated (below) will almost double the cost.

Expanding Production

5$\frac{1}{2}$-gallon (25-litre) bucket

These buckets are usually made from polyethylene, polypropylene or rigid PVC. For winemaking they should be of high density food grade material, which has considerable resistance to staining and does not easily acquire 'off' flavours. More importantly there is no danger of toxins being leached out. Those specifically made for wine and beermaking are best as they are supplied with a tight-fitting, snap-on lid and have a number of uses, including that of a primary fermenter. The first, vigorous stage of a fermentation, particularly a pulp fermentation, should be undertaken in such a vessel before transfer to a carboy. Two such buckets are therefore recommended. They are quite cheap and readily available from all good homebrew suppliers, and from Boots, Woolworths etc.

One of the buckets illustrated (above) has a hole bored in its lid so that a standard bung carrying a heater and airlock can be fitted for its use as a fermenter. When not required the hole is merely plugged with an unbored bung.

Walker Desmond Pulpmaster

When making the larger wine batches, particularly using summer fruits, a few items of more sophisticated equipment are very useful. In this category the Walker Desmond Pulpmaster is certainly good value and is virtually everlasting. Large quantities of fruit or vegetables can be pulped very quickly and cleanly; a load of apples can be pulped in as little as 10 seconds simply by connecting the impeller drive spindle to any handyman's drill. The complete unit contains one cutting blade and spindle, white nylon-coated metal cover, spindle bearing and 2-gallon (10-litre) plastic bucket. Essentially, these pulpers are used to break down hard fruits before fermentation on the pulp or pressing. For very large quantities or especially hard fruits, crushers are sometimes used, and though these are very effective, they are really outside the volume and price range of those to whom this book is directed. The Pulpmaster is a very satisfactory and inexpensive alternative.

Walker Desmond wine press

This unit is really intended as a stablemate of the Pulpmaster. It is used to extract the juice from the softer fruits and also from harder fruits following pulping. It is very useful for expressing juice from pulp immediately following removal from the must. This press operates on the screw principle, in which a fine pitch screw is used to drive a heavy pressure plate down the centre of a perforated cylinder containing the fruit or pulp. This particular design is in steel and cast iron, being rendered suitable for winemaking by a heavy nylon coating. Thus it is particularly easy to clean whilst being inexpensive to buy.

Similar models made by other manufacturers are also available. This type of press is relatively efficient and, being inexpensive, is likely to be the type finding its way into the private winemaker's possession.

There is another type of press, known as the 'rack and cloth', in which a number of cloth or canvas envelopes are filled with pulp and built up alternately with wooden dividing racks. This type is somewhat more complex to set up but is highly efficient in extracting the maximum of juice. This type lends itself better to home construction by the handyman, being essentially of wood and often operated by a hydraulic car jack as the means of applying great pressure.

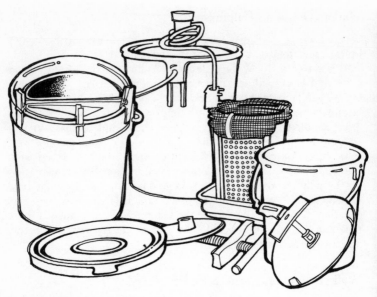

Equipment Rigged for Production Operations

SUMMING UP

This concludes the coverage of winemaking equipment, so perhaps it is fitting to end the chapter rather as it began — by mentioning in a very general way the equipment which is not necessarily only for winemaking. At the outset, mention was made of some very general items to be found in the kitchen. Simple and virtually essential. There are, however, many items available today which one could not describe as essential, even though highly desirable and often quite expensive. If these are available so much the better and there is certainly no reason why their use should not be extended to embrace winemaking. In particular, a variety of juice extractors, both hand and power operated, such as the Kenwood and others, can certainly take the labour out of juice preparation, especially for making the lighter white wines.

And of course, there are pressure cookers, steam juice extractors and large scale boilers. All have their uses and many authors advocate them, but frankly I prefer, where possible, to avoid the use of any form of boiler or steamer for winemaking. Heating and cooling is both expensive and time consuming and excessive heating for juice extraction can cause cooked flavours and hazes.

CHAPTER 6

PREPARING MUSTS FOR FERMENTATION

According to Dr Peter McCall in his *Winemaker's Dictionary*, the definition of a must is that 'it is the prepared juice from the time of its preparation until the end of fermentation, when it may be called (if not considered to be) wine'. He states that the word is derived from the Latin *mustus*, meaning new. It will be seen from the simple equation at the beginning of Chapter Two that this prepared juice is represented by fruit flavouring which, when using the fruits available to us, invariably requires extension with water and sugar. In order to render these juices suitable for fermentation, other additions also need to be made for the benefit of finished taste and to aid the fermentation process.

The preparation of the must and its fermentations are arguably the two most important factors in winemaking. Get these right and you will be well on the way to success. When preparing the must, the importance of getting things balanced correctly at the outset cannot be overstressed. Each of the ingredients and additions have an important role to play, and can best perform their part if present in the correct form and quantity during the fermentation stage. One should guard, so far as possible, against making additions after fermentation, though one or two minor adjustments, mainly concerning sweetness and acidity, may be desirable.

Yeast multiplies and becomes active much more quickly when closely confined and therefore the best way of inoculating a must is to prepare a small fermentation (a yeast starter) some 24 hours or more before its intended use. Preparing the yeast starter is simplicity itself and should cause no inconvenience.

All fruit musts, other than commercially prepared wine concentrates, need to be prepared in two distinct stages, again at least 24 hours apart so that the prepared juice or pulp may be sterilized by 'sulphiting' before the final stages of preparation and inoculation.

For convenience, it is common practice to make up the yeast starter and prepare the juice or pulp in one session, balancing the must and inoculating it with the starter some 24 hours or so later. Commercially prepared wine concentrates do not need the sulphite treatment and can be made up and inoculated in one session. However, in such cases it is still advisable to use a starter and this must, of course, be made up some 24 hours or more earlier, as outlined.

There are a number of ways of making up a yeast starter and those described in Chapter Seven are satisfactory for all the recipes advocated in this book. Choose that which is most convenient.

JUICE VERSUS PULP FERMENTATION

Preparing grape musts commercially has already been briefly touched upon, outlining how white wines are usually the result of juice fermentation whilst the heavier red wines are normally the result of some degree of pulp fermentation in order to extract colouring from the fruit skins. It is a fact that white grape wines can be made from red grapes if juice fermentation is undertaken and the skins removed, as the colouring of grapes is only skin deep. However, in using our own fruits, these boundaries are not nearly so closely defined, nor do they need to be. Generally speaking, regardless of colour, wines fermented on the pulp will be somewhat more robust, will have more body and may be somewhat more difficult to clear, whilst those produced purely from juice will tend to be smoother and lighter. These latter lend themselves to table wines, particularly the white variety. Pulp fermentation requires rather less equipment and in some cases, due to the nature of the fruit, a little pulp fermentation may be necessary to break down the fruit structure and thus improve juice yield before subsequently pressing and continuing as a juice fermentation. Apples are an important case in point, since apples are a fruit much used in home winemaking. Of course, in all cases, all our wines revert to juice fermentation when the pulp is removed from the must after a number of days.

Colouring of our home fruit wines, as well as being derived from materials contained in the skin, may originate from the fruit juice itself, as occurs with blackberries.

Today we use different methods of extracting the juice from those that were once popular. Years ago almost invariably the fruits were boiled, or boiling water was added prior to fermentation with the two-fold purpose of sterilization and assisting in juice extraction.

42

Though these methods are still sometimes practised today they have considerable disadvatanges, and sterilization is far better achieved by sulphiting. Boiling often produces a 'cooked' flavour and is also very detrimental in that it de-natures the pectin-destroying enzymes whilst simultaneously increasing the extraction of natural pectin from the fruit. Pectin is a component of the fruit cell walls which is brought into solution by boiling and is the feature used to advantage in jam-making to cause it to set. In winemaking excess pectin will cause stubborn hazes in finished wines, so pectin-destroying enzymes should be added to all musts.

Even the use of boiled water, often advocated, can be detrimental and is quite unnecessary as boiling greatly reduces the dissolved oxygen content of the water which is so necessary in the early stages of fermentation.

Water from the cold water tap is ideally suited to our purpose. If, for some reason, water boiling has to be undertaken, the water should be stirred vigorously and preferably 'churned' after cooling and before use, so as to absorb fresh oxygen from the air. In such cases it is assumed that boiling will be undertaken to remove certain elements from the water rather than for sterilization purposes.

To sum up, provided the equipment is available, juice fermentation is to be preferred, especially for the lighter white table wines. They are easier to control and more accuracy can be exercised in sugar and acid assessment at the outset, thereby making it easier to assess what additions need to be made. This is not necessarily so when working to a recipe as quantities will be specified but it is most useful when devising one's own recipes.

JUICE AND PULP ORIGINS
Commercially Prepared Wine Concentrates

Most wines in this category will be juice fermentations, especially the grape wines which predominate, though there are a few country wines which need to be regarded as pulp types. This applies particularly to America, where country fruit wine concentrates are far more common than in Europe. Throughout Europe today there are a number of kit manufacturers, offering products which make home wine simplicity itself. These are of great benefit to the beginner who can get a very good insight into the craft by their use. They also have a very real interest for the more experienced operator, not merely because of their simplicity but also because they are capable of producing very acceptable wines, especially the table variety, quickly and at a relatively low cost.

43

There are also concentrates available for making wines which need virtually no maturing whatsoever — often called 'quickie' wines — and these are of particular interest to the beginner who naturally has no stock of finished wines upon which to draw. However, artificial ageing and maturing are no real substitute for the natural processes of time.

Concentrates are available in a variety of qualities, concentrations and prices and also to make a range of finished quantities. As in most matters, the best results tend to stem from the best quality products and, having in mind the additional costs in sugar and time, it certainly pays to opt for quality. In general it is best to follow the manufacturer's instructions. However, for simplicity some recommend adding all of the make-up sugar at the outset whilst others advocate adding a proportion at the start and the remainder some time later as fermentation proceeds. I prefer the latter method, regardless of manufacturer, as this aids the fermentation process.

It is quite normal, especially for beginners, to make up concentrates in the actual fermentation vessel or demijohn from the start, but use of a suitably sized winemaking bucket in the initial stage has distinct advantages, especially if the initial fermentation becomes very vigorous as is frequently the case.

Concentrates based on country wines are similarly handled, excepting that it is generally necessary to remove the pulp debris after a time according to the manufacturer's instructions. The use of a bucket in the initial stages of fermentation in these instances is clearly apparent.

Fresh, Canned and Bottled Fruits

Wines under this heading can be produced from either juice or pulp musts according to the nature of the fruit and the equipment available. This book is primarily intended for those making wines in this category, and I feel sure you will derive the greatest satisfaction, both in initial achievement and final enjoyment, from them. Many beginners who start with concentrates will wish to graduate to wines in this category and especially to the wines employing fresh fruits in their season. Alternatively, it is hoped that this book is sufficiently clear for newcomers to start at this point omitting concentrates altogether if they so wish. Such wines can be produced by either juice or pulp fermentation, and the choice should be made bearing in mind what has already been said about characteristics, colour and availability of equipment.

As dealt with earlier, certain strains of grape make the best commercial wines. Accordingly, it has become increasingly popular in recent years to incorporate some of this fruit, in one form or other, in all our fruit wines, and most modern recipes will include this feature. This is most beneficial for, in adding a quantity of grape, we not only improve fermentation by adding many essential nutrients, but we also provide a measure of that important quality called 'body'. It is usual to add it either in the form of grape concentrate or minced sultanas or raisins which are dried white and red grapes respectively.

Grape concentrate can be added to both juice and pulp musts, but minced sultanas and raisins should only be added to pulp musts as they provide some pulp. In performance there is no real reason why we should not add the dried fruit to prepared juices, but this tends to defeat the object of juice preparation because the minced fruit needs to be removed after a few days of fermentation. White grape juice or sultanas should be used for white wines but either red or white juice, raisins or sultanas, may be used for the red varieties. Red concentrate added to white wines such as those based on apples tends to produce a most delicate rosé according to the amount used, whilst if added to a 'yellow' white, such as that derived from oranges, produces a rather off-putting orange-coloured beverage. These anticipated colours are important to consider, since colour in a wine is as important as both taste and bouquet.

First, decide the quantity of wine to be made and thoroughly wash and clean a plastic winemaking bucket of sufficient size, finally rinsing it with a little 1% sodium metabisulphite solution made up as described in Chapter Four. Next, add to the bucket 1 pint (570 ml) of water and one teaspoon of 10% stock sodium metabisulphite solution for each finished gallon (5 litres). For instance, if 5 gallons (23 litres) are to be made, add 5 pints (2.85 litres) of water and 5 teaspoons (25 ml) of 10% sodium metabisulphite solution. It will be recalled that 1 teaspoon (5 ml) of the strong sulphite solution is equivalent to one campden tablet and so one tablet per finished gallon (5 litres) may be added if preferred. The tablets must be crushed and thoroughly dissolved in a little warmed water before being stirred into the water in the bucket.

The solution thus formed in the bucket constitutes a 24 hour sterilizing agent for the prepared fruit which must be added either as a pulp or juice and left to stand for this period prior to commencement of fermentation. During this time the sodium metabisulphite will have done its job, and in so doing will have lost sufficient potency as to have little or no detrimental effect on the yeast when it is added. In the meantime, the bucket lid must be firmly fitted, being removed only in order to make additions of fruit as it is prepared.

According to the recipe being followed, it is an easy matter to determine the amount of fruit required and the amount of grape concentrate, sultanas or raisins, for the chosen batch size. If sultanas or raisins are to be included they should be thoroughly washed and minced, or finely chopped and added to the above sulphite solution immediately following its preparation, followed by the fruit as detailed below. Alternatively, if it is intended to use grape concentrate, this need not be added immediately but may, if you wish, be added when the final adjustments are made to the must.

Soft Fruits

Thoroughly wash the fruit in small batches to remove all dirt, crop sprays, livestock and discard any which is mouldy, rotting or potentially suspect in any way. With the larger fruits cut out any signs of damage or bruising.

Larger fruits such as peaches and apricots should first be stoned, whichever method of fermentation is chosen, and this is also desirable for the smaller fruits such as plums and damsons if the stones are easily removable. If, however, the stones tend to be stubborn and it is not practicable to remove them, employ a pulp fermentation, in which case each fruit should merely be broken by hand before adding to the sterilant in the bucket. The stones should be removed later if the fruit is to be pressed. If damsons or Victoria plums are your main ingredient for a red wine, pulp fermentation will be necessary anyway in order that colouring may be extracted from the skins.

If you have kitchen equipment capable of juicing the fruit and thereby separating the stones in this way, then by all means use it.

Smaller fruits containing seeds such as elderberries can be pressed satisfactorily, but in the case of elderberries only a light rosé is obtainable in this way and they are not particularly easy to juice. If a deep red wine is required from elderberries then pulp fermentation will be necessary; they must be thoroughly crushed in a bowl first, by a block of wood or similar before adding to the sterilant. Very soft fruits such as blackberries and raspberries crush very readily to pulp and are treated as a pulp fermentation.

Pulp fermentation plays a large part in home winemaking, either because of a lack of the more sophisticated equipment or as a way of extracting the colour of some fruits. Certainly, it should not be avoided, for although juice fermentation is more refined and better suited to table wines, many progressive amateurs have a preference, rightly or wrongly, for the fuller bodied type. These are naturally quite popularly produced on the pulp basis.

Hard Fruits

The same comments regarding inspection and cleanliness apply here. In the case of apples and pears there is no requirement to peel or core them. If the chosen fruits are of a relatively bland nature and contain considerable juice, they can be used to make high quality wines with very little need for water in the final adjustment. But a good wine can be obtained when using two parts juice to one part water and this has certain advantages when dissolving the sugar. Apples and pears are the principal contenders here and they lend themselves especially to white wine production, including the table variety, because it is relatively easy to obtain a good, transparent juice. Again, due to the generally bland nature of these fruits, the sharper-tasting varieties are considered best and in this latter respect apples are better than pears. Pears are best used mixed with apples or some other fruit, and so far as apples are concerned, these should be a mixture of a cooking and dessert variety, perhaps with the cooking type predominating.

To express the juice really economically a fruit press or juice extractor is necessary, and the fruit must first be pulped in some way. This can be done by cutting the fruit into slices or chunks and crushing, or if larger quantities are involved, by use of a crushing machine. However, crushers are very expensive and for the amounts of fruit involved in home production, even on the larger scale, the Pulpmaster as advocated in Chapter Five and illustrated at plate five is a much cheaper alternative. If a press is used following pulping, the pulp should be pressed in a fine filter bag. After sulphiting for 24 hours before fermentation it is usually quite a simple matter to strain off the juice from the well-defined residual pulp layer.

A method I have used successfully with apples if a crusher or pulper is not available, is to place the apples in a deep freeze overnight, allowing them to thaw thoroughly before working with them the next day. In this way expansion of the water in the fruit during freezing tends to rupture the cell structure of the apples, so that when thawed they are extremely soft and easier to press. But allow them to thaw thoroughly; if the centres are still frozen when you press them much of the juice will be lost.

Alternatively pulp fermentation is a possibility and, again, the use of a crusher or the Pulpmaster is ideal. In fact, a short pulp fermentation after pulping helps to break down the cell walls and achieve maximum juice yield when the pulp is pressed.

As in the case of soft fruits, additions of stock campden solution and pectolytic enzyme will be necessary, as will the 24 hour steriliz-ing period. The use of a campden solution immediately following pulping is essential for hard fruits which otherwise would tend to oxidize and turn brown. However, with such fruits, water additions should be kept to a minimum or may even be omitted at this stage, especially if a high proportion of fruit is being used. Otherwise it is possible to end up with too much must when the necessary addi-tions, including sugar, have been made. This fault tends to result in a messy initial fermentation, particularly if the pulp method has been employed.

Citrus Fruits

Juice fermentation is favourite here. All that is necessary is to cut the fruit across its centre and squeeze out the juice, using a fruit juicer as shown on page 26. Alternatively peel the fruit and then use an electric juicer or fruit press. Another alternative is to purchase large cans of ready prepared, pure unsweetened juice from the supermarket. In this convenient form the juice is ready to use, but often such recipes advocate an addition of some 'bite' to the wine by including juice from lemons or from Seville marmalade oranges which are only available in the shops during January/February. These are dealt with as described above, and often some of the outer peel is also included in the must by finely peeling some of the fruit using a sharpened potato/apple peeler. But these parings must be very thin (resembling peel from an apple) and on no account must the white pith of citrus fruits be included in a must, as this causes an unpleasant and quite unacceptable bitter taste in the finished wine which cannot be removed.

As the juice is prepared it is added to the campden solution, the pectolytic enzyme is added and the bucket is tightly covered for 24 hours, as for soft and hard fruit preparations.

Dried Fruits

Dried fruits cannot be successfully prepared as a juice fermentation. By their very nature they contain no free-running juice. To prepare them for pulp fermentation they must first be washed and soaked, then minced or chopped before adding to the metabisulphite and pectolytic enzyme solution for 24 hours.

THE ADDITIONS

At this point it is assumed that the prepared juice, or pulp in solution, with metabisulphite and pectolytic enzyme, has stood for 24 to 36 hours and that an adequate yeast starter is available which is vigorously active and ready to go. However, before adding the starter the must has to be made up with the following additions and extended as necessary with water.

Pectolytic Enzyme and Amylase

In consideration of all the additions to the prepared juice or must, pectolytic enzyme and possibly amylase, if starch difficulties are envisaged, are the only items which should already have been added at this stage. If, for some reason, they were omitted during preparation, add them without further delay.

Fruits containing pectin also bear their own natural enzymes in order to break it down but they may be insufficient for winemaking purposes, and as it is so important to eliminate pectin from wine the addition of pectolytic enzyme should be routine. It is certainly better to add it at the outset than to deal with the hazes which can result from its omission.

Pectolytic enzyme is usually obtainable from homebrew shops and chemists under this name but there are also proprietary names such as Pectinol and Pectolase. Some are liquid and some are in powdered form; both work equally well. Use either according to manufacturer's instructions.

Amylase is similarly provided, according to manufacturer's instructions, and should be used when the must ingredients have a high starch level, e.g. apples. The amylase will break down the starch and prevent a haze forming.

Water and Sugar

Our finished wines contain between 80 and 90% water, with most of the sugar added earlier having been converted to ethyl alcohol. We must now, therefore, extend the prepared juice with water and add at least a proportion of the sugar in order to be able to set the process in motion.

The initial fermentation should be conducted in the bucket to provide sufficient air and room to allow the vigorous effervescence to take place. If you elect to perform a juice fermentation in the demijohn do not add all the water at this stage, but allow an air space of about 2 pints (1 litre) to remain; this will allow the froth to rise in the jar without travelling up into the airlock.

All of the sugar should not be provided initially as fermentation starts best when there is an optimum amount of sugar in a must and this is when its content is in the order of 1¼ lb (560 g) per gallon (5 litres). Increase or decrease this amount and fermentation is retarded. However, the actual amount to be provided initially is not critical but, remembering that the juice or pulp itself contains sugar, as does the grape or sultanas, I have found it most practical to add initially sufficient sugar to bring the total starting amount to within 1 lb (450 g) of that finally intended. Table wines call for rather less sugar than the dessert style but in either case make a habit of omitting the final 1 lb (450 g).

Hence, we can make-up the final amount in all cases for each finished gallon (5 litres) by progressive feeding in to it 1 pint (570 ml) of strong sugar syrup (SSS). To make this, 2 lb (900 g) are dissolved in 1 pint (570 ml) of water, assisted by warming but *not* boiling to make 2 pints (1 litre) of syrup.

So, as an example, assume a 5-gallon (23-litre) batch is to be produced. All that is necessary is to dissolve 5 lb (2.27 kg) of sugar in 2½ pints (1.43 litres) of water by very gently warming (not boiling) in a saucepan to make a strong sugar solution (SSS) and, when cooled, transfer it to a demijohn or similar vessel and fit a stopper. This may then be used as a feed as fermentation proceeds and sugar is converted to alcohol. Subtract this amount of sugar from the amount in the recipe and the remainder must be dissolved into the bulk of the must for the initial part of the fermentation. Again, to do this, warm it with a little water in a saucepan and add to the prepared juice when cool.

The bulk, when you are ready to commence fermentation, should have a temperature of around 70 to 75°F (21 to 24°C). This is the ideal temperature at which to commence fermentation. However, the temperature should not be allowed to rise above 80°F (27°C) once the pectolytic enzyme has been added, nor should a starter be added to a must having a temperature above 75°F (24°C).

When publishing a wine recipe, the originator can only specify the sugar and other additions which need to be made based on known average figures for the ingredients which will be used. Quite obviously he or she has no way of knowing exactly the sugar or acid content of the fruits that others are proposing to use. In a poor summer fruits will tend to be low in sugar and high in acid but in a good summer the reverse will be true. There is no need to worry unduly about this as the fruits having a high acid content often make the better wine, but it is nevertheless most important that these two items in particular need to be correctly balanced in any given wine style. For this reason it is better and far more satisfying if we are able to measure the sugar and acid content of our musts so that we can assess more accurately for ourselves the adjustments which need to be made. Chapters Eleven and Twelve deal with these aspects and both are equally simple and inexpensive to perform.

However, in working to a given recipe large errors are not likely to be involved and it matters little if our table wines range between 10 and 12% alcohol and the dessert variety between 15 and 17% without our knowledge of any greater accuracy. The amount of sugar and fruit in a dessert wine is always greater for not only must there be a higher alcohol content but the finished wine must also be sweeter and the sweetness and extra flavour will need to be balanced with acid.

Acidity Adjustments

For years there has been continuing disagreement among enthusiasts about wine acids and the subtle complexities of chemical improvements which can be caused by these acids during fermentation and ageing. Quite a number of acids are being used these days by advanced winemakers, but there are three acids in particular which have been used for many years by amateurs and will no doubt be used by them for many years to come. These are the three fruit acids and are specified below. Some advocate the use of one and some another whilst others advocate the use of a mixture of two or three. This latter course is a good idea, for the underlying characteristics of each acid are well known and so a mixture not only imparts an overall final acid strength, but each confers its own special contribution to the whole.

Each of these three acids are fruit acids and need to be considered individually. For example, in an orange wine we may feel it best to omit additions of the acid known to predominate in oranges and make up any difference required by use of one or other or both of the remaining two. These acids, which can all be readily purchased in crystalline form from most chemists and homebrew suppliers, are all of differing strength and so in substituting one acid for another, it may be necessary to adjust the amount accordingly. Chapter Twelve discusses the method of acid assessment by titration. Appendix I shows the normally recommended acid levels for various wine styles and Appendix II shows the conversion relationship from one acid to another.

The relatively small amounts of acid called for in the recipe must be weighed out reasonably accurately using, for example, the Dr

51

Oetker balance as specified in Chapter Five and illustrated on page 35, or as tabulated in Appendix I. The measured acid must be dissolved in a very small quantity of warm water and stirred into the must. In some cases the acid in the fruit itself may be sufficient without any further additions, and in some instances the high level of acid in the fruit may limit the amount of fruit used in order to keep the acid level within acceptable limits.

In addition to contributing to the finished taste of a wine, and also to maturation, acids in general greatly aid fermentation, and they act as a minor sterilant, preventing the formation of off-flavours.

The requisite amount of acid should always be added before fermentation begins, rather than at a later date. Of course, a little adjustment may be desirable prior to bottling, particularly if it is intended to mature the wine over a protracted period. Some adjustment may also be necessary in the case of pulp fermentation, where it is more difficult to assess the total acid content at the outset.

Citric Acid
This is the main acid in citrus fruits such as oranges, lemons and grapefruit. Among amateurs it is undoubtedly the most popular of the fruit acids. It is added to many commercially prepared fruit drinks and concentrates and is the acid popularly used in boiled sweets. It is a favourite for taste, and included in our wines is no exception. It aids a vigorous fermentation and citrus fruits are highly fermentable. However, citric acid is of little value to the maturing process and either some other fruit acid in combination, or the acid intrinsic in another fruit in combination will be needed to make a further contribution.

Tartaric Acid
This is the acid found in grapes, and as they are regarded as being ideal for winemaking, tartaric acid is considered to be highly desirable in quality wines. This acid is particularly useful in maturation, creating ester forming reactions. Esters are the result of complex chemical reactions, imparting both bouquet and flavour qualities to a wine. Accordingly, some winemakers advocate its use exclusively. Another virtue is that it can be easily reduced by chilling the wine in a refrigerator. Should the final acid level be too high, chilling causes this acid to partially precipitate out of solution as potassium hydrogen tartrate crystals. The wine can then be decanted, leaving the crystals behind.

Malic Acid
This is the principal acid to be found in apples, the name of which is

derived from the Latin, *malum* — an apple. It is, however, also to be found in grapes, particularly those grown in more Northern climates where the fruit never becomes particularly sweet. The acid itself tends to be rather bitter and probably for this reason it is the least popular of the three acids. It is better used in conjunction with another, but its value in ester formation should not be overlooked as it helps produce good bouquet and flavour.

Tannin

The presence of tannin in a wine gives it astringency, which produces an element of dryness in the mouth when drinking. In a moderate amount it is highly desirable, particularly in red wines, but home wines often contain far too much, particularly the elderberry, apple and plum varieties. It is generally to be found in the skins of the fruit, so it tends to abound in pulp fermentations.

Tannin can be added, and grape tannin is readily available to home winemakers as either powder or in solution. To some extent, the quantity required must be added to suit as it is not possible for the amateur to measure the content.

Fortunately, tannin levels reduce as maturation proceeds. In years gone by tannin was the compound provided by additions of cold tea to a must but please, not for musts as recommended here!

Yeast Nutrient and Energizers

Lastly, in consideration that yeast is a living organism, it is highly desirable to add nutrient and energizers to the must, just as fertilizers are added to soil to promote healthy and vigorous growth. This facet alone could promote discussion and consideration well outside the terms of reference of this book, as a complex of trace elements are involved. However, if musts are made up as already described, a number of these trace elements will always be present, and the home winemaker is again well catered for these days as cheap proprietary additions are readily available.

Essentially, yeast requires ammonium salts as a nutrient, the cheapest and most popular appearing to be ammonium sulphate but there is a trend today towards ammonium phosphate. Either will do the job and indeed, some preparations contain both. Potassium is another requirement and potassium phosphate is a very important nutrient, the inclusion of which will do much to prevent a 'stuck' fermentation. In soft water areas a very small quantity of magnesium sulphate (Epsom salts) is useful.

All of these additives can be purchased in convenient form from homebrew suppliers, appropriately called nutrient tablets.

In addition to these trace elements it is becoming increasingly popular to add vitamins, by way of a 3 mg tablet per gallon (5 litres) of thiamine hydrochloride (aneurine hydrochloride.) If purchased from a chemist they may be marketed under either name but if acquired from a home wine outlet they will be called vitamin B_1 tablets. They are obtainable in a variety of milligram sizes, i.e. 3, 10 and 15 mg, but it is an easy matter to assess one's total requirement and maybe break down a larger tablet for lesser quantities.

Instead of compounding our own, comprehensive nutrient salts combining energizers may now be obtained, and these are particularly good for dessert wines in which one desires a really high alcohol content. A typical example is the yeast nutrient and energizer known as Tronozymol.

In all cases tablets should be crushed first and all powders well dissolved in a little water before adding to the must. Use only the quantity stated in the recipe or, in the case of proprietary preparations, the amount advocated in the instructions. As fermentation proceeds, these additives tend to become exhausted by the yeast. Overdoses will result in a residual quantity, which will not improve the finished taste of the wine.

So, having prepared the concentrate, juice or pulp to your choice according to the fruit source available and as outlined above, and having made the necessary additions, you have completed preparation of the must. You should have adjusted the temperature of the bulk to within 70 to 75°F (21 to 24°C) when you made the initial sugar additions and you will also have an active yeast starter available.

It now only remains to add this starter to the must and maintain temperature in order to initiate and sustain a healthy and vigorous fermentation.

SUMMING UP

1. Preferably commence initial fermentation in a bucket for both fruit juices and pulps.
2. Add all juice or pulp to campden or sulphite solution in a bucket immediately it is prepared. Keep the bucket covered.
3. Add grape juice, sultanas or raisins to pulp fermentations, but only grape juice to juice fermentation.
4. Add red or white grape juice, sultanas or raisins to red wines but only white grape juice or sultanas to white wines unless a rosé effect is required.
5. If sultanas or raisins are being added they should be thoroughly washed before mincing.
6. Immediately the juice or pulp is prepared, add pectolytic enzyme as a matter of habit and amylase if necessary.
7. Avoid boiling fruit and use of boiling water wherever possible.
8. Add only part of the sugar to start with, making later additions of strong sugar solution.
9. Try to assess the acid requirements of the wine you are making and use the wine acid or acids best suited.
10. Do not forget the yeast nutrients and energizers and add according to supplier's instructions.

CHAPTER 7

FERMENTATION — THE TRANSITION TO WINE

YEASTS AND YEAST STARTERS

At the beginning of the previous chapter, mention was made of preparing the yeast starter and the need for this to be the first task when making a batch of wine. Accordingly, before looking into the matter of fermentation in greater depth, here are the methods I recommend for the starter and which I have always found to be successful. They are suitable for any winemaking activity.

The initial choice and nurturing of the yeast throughout fermentation is of the utmost importance for, if the yeast colony is well developed and healthy, fermentation should cause no problems. Only wine yeasts should be used and not baker's or brewer's yeasts. The former is specifically suited to breadmaking and is extremely active in the very early stages, giving off large volumes of carbon dioxide (CO_2) over a very short period which, whilst being what bakers require, is certainly not suitable for our own purpose. The latter is only suitable for beermaking. Furthermore, neither is capable of producing a particularly high level of alcohol.

Today, winemaking yeasts for the amateur are available in many forms and styles and in a bewildering variety bearing the names of many famous commercial wine producing areas. Others are famous in their own right as general purpose yeasts such as Formula 67 marketed by Continental Wine Experts Ltd., Southern Vinyards' 'Vin kwik' and the quite extraordinary Gervin Wine Yeasts marketed by Gervin Supplies. Many are also available in liquid form and some people prefer these, but the dried forms today give such good results and are so convenient to use that most beginners quite naturally appear to opt for these. What has already been said implies that these yeasts are produced essentially from the grape and many claims are made which may suggest to the newcomer that use of a certain named yeast is likely to produce its own distinctive product flavour and characteristics quite regardless of the particular must to which it is applied. It will not. Suffice it to say that use of a particular yeast will help if one is making up a concentrate claiming to be of that particular commercial wine origin, or perhaps if one is making a serious attempt at a given result.

To give serious thought to the matter of choice however, helps in other ways. For instance, if one is making up a juice fermentation for a delicate table wine of low alcohol content one may well choose a Bernkastler, Niersteiner or Bordeaux yeast since these are essentially of that particular style. Certainly there would be little point in using a yeast known to be related to a very robust style of dessert — otherwise, should there be a little residual sweetening sugar, fermentation may well recommence after bottling. Conversely, it would not be logical to use a yeast related to a delicate wine style if a really robust dessert style were intended. In such cases it would be better to use a Port, Tarragona or Tokay type of yeast.

As fermentation takes place its rate slows, particularly in the early stages, not so much because the sugar content of the must is dwindling, but because the increasing alcohol content gradually inhibits yeast activity; provided enough sugar is present, the alcohol content will finally inhibit activity completely. Obviously, a yeast of known low alcohol tolerance would be unsuitable here. In fact, apart from the fruit quantity put into a must, the essential differences between table and dessert styles have just been considered.

Unless sold in quantity, dried yeasts are usually supplied in small packs for starting a bulk of about 2 to 5 gallons (10 to 23 litres) and if one is only contemplating making 1 gallon (5 litres) it is sometimes advocated that the yeast be merely added to the main bulk and stirred in. However, even for 1 gallon (5 litres), this is not the way to operate and for larger quantities there is a distinct possibility of failure. Remember, one cannot really afford to wait for failure and a good fermenting yeast should be ready and waiting to inoculate the body of the must immediately it is finally made up.

The best method of preparing a yeast starter is to take a standard wine bottle, preferably of clear glass, and thoroughly rinse it, using running water and a bottle brush. Next, express the juice from a medium-sized orange into a measuring jug and add to it one dessertspoon of sugar, a quarter teaspoon of citric acid and one crushed 3 mg vitamin B_1 tablet. Add about a cupful of warmed water (not hot or boiled) and thoroughly mix until the sugar and acid have dissolved. Pour this carefully into the bottle and adjust the water in the bottle, to approximately just over half full, with slightly warmed water to provide a finished temperature of 70 to 75°F (21 to 24°C). If the temperature is above 75°F (24°C) allow to cool to this value before pouring in the yeast from the packet. Shake thoroughly to disperse the yeast and plug the bottle with cotton wool (not a cork!). On no account must yeast be added at temperatures above 80°F (27°C).

Alternatively, if you are preparing a juice fermentation, a little of this juice may be taken, instead of expressing the juice from an orange, and dealt with in the same way. In this case, however, one needs to be careful, especially when using fruit such as apples, which browns when exposed to air, for as the juice is required for fermentation right away, it must not be sulphited as advocated for the main bulk. I prefer the use of a separate orange, for the addition of this amount of flavouring to any must, even though it be only 1 gallon (5 litres) is of no consequence and certainly will not impair the quality or taste of any finished wine. Additionally, as oranges contain citric acid they are highly fermentable and a vigorous starter is what is needed.

Having adjusted the temperature and added the yeast, for whichever method you have chosen, the temperature of the starter must now be maintained until it is fed into the must. Writers often imply that the starter be placed somewhere warm, having a steady and continuous temperature in the range 70 to 75°F (21 to 24°C). What they do not tell us is where, in the home, we are likely to find such conditions and indeed such a place is far more difficult to find than one would imagine. This will be dealt with later in the chapter when maintaining fermentation warmth is discussed.

After the elapse of some 24 to 36 hours, and when the prepared juice has been extended to produce the must with its additions as already outlined, the yeast starter may be added — but first check that it is really active. This should not be difficult to determine as it may already have 'blown its top' by pushing free the cotton wool plug, but if not, take the bottle of starter and, holding it at chest height, swirl it around. Next, turn the bottle to an angle of 45° by moving the neck away from you. If a steady stream of bubbles appear to travel up the sloping side of the bottle facing your eye then the starter is active and can be added right away to the must. If you have worked according to the previous chapter in preparing the must, it too will be at the correct fermentation temperature and this must be maintained. If so, you can await developments, but do not expect anything at all for at least a few hours.

PRINCIPLES OF FERMENTATION

All forms of life need energy and all energy originates from the sun. Plants capture the energy and store it as carbohydrates; animals and certain other plants such as yeast liberate the stored energy to form carbon dioxide and water.

When completely burned, one atom of carbon (C) combines with two atoms of oxygen (O) from the air to form one molecule of carbon dioxide (CO_2), and two atoms of hydrogen (H) combine with one atom of oxygen (O) to form one molecule of water (H_2O). When these elements combine with oxygen thereby giving up heat and are no longer able to combine further, no more oxidation can take place. They are then said to be in their highest oxidation state. It is interesting to note that both water and carbon dioxide are the two compounds most commonly used in firefighting.

It has been found that a ready grown yeast colony will continue to thrive in a must by combining *some* of the oxygen that the sugar contains with the carbon that the same compound contains if free air is not available. Hence, when a yeast is introduced into a must a colony will grow very quickly whilst consuming the dissolved air present in the water and, when this is expended, will continue to thrive by an anaerobic (without air) transmode of life, utilizing the oxygen chemically combined in the sugar. This is the reason water for musts should not be boiled, as this drives off the oxygen which permits initial expansion of the colony. In the anaerobic mode, a quantity of carbon dioxide is continually released and the remaining elements left behind combine to form molecules of another substance — ethyl alcohol.

So, in subtracting a few carbon, hydrogen and oxygen atoms from sugar in the form we know it, another substance is formed totally different in appearance if not so different in chemical composition. A clear liquid which happily has a very distinctive effect on our senses; it is quite different from sugar itself, but it becomes easy to see why those on a diet who must restrict their sugar intake must also restrict alcohol consumption.

Let us now take another look at the basic winemaking equation given at the beginning of Chapter Two in an effort to clarify what has already been said. It will be seen that item one is identical with item four and also that two and five are common to both sides of the equation. For the purpose of this exercise, therefore, the scales, or equation, will still balance if we remove these items completely to write the equation thus:

$$\text{Sugar} \xrightarrow[\text{(Fermentation)}]{\text{Yeast added}} \text{Ethyl alcohol + carbon dioxide}$$

Written chemically this simple but very famous formula is attributed to the French scientist Gay-Lussac who discovered it early in the 19th century, before the role of yeast in fermentation had been established.

$$\begin{array}{ccc} \text{Sugar} & \text{(Fermentation)} & \text{Ethyl} + \text{carbon} \\ \text{(glucose)} & & \text{alcohol} \quad \text{dioxide} \\ C_6H_{12}O_6 & \longrightarrow & 2C_2H_5OH \quad 2CO_2 \end{array}$$

Granulated sugar, sucrose, has the formula $C_{12}H_{22}O_{11}$ and this is first broken down by the yeast to two simpler sugars

$$\begin{array}{cccc} C_{12}H_{22}O_{11} + H_2O & \longrightarrow & C_6H_{12}O_6 & + & C_6H_{12}O_6 \\ \text{SUCROSE} & & \text{GLUCOSE} & & \text{FRUCTOSE} \end{array}$$

From the above it can be deduced that every molecule of glucose containing six atoms of carbon (C), twelve atoms of hydrogen (H) and six atoms of oxygen (O), when acted upon by yeast fermentation with outside air excluded, causes four atoms of carbon and two atoms of oxygen to be broken away to form two molecules of carbon dioxide gas (CO_2). This escapes through the airlock on top of the fermentation vessel (or in the initial stages from around the bucket lid) leaving behind two molecules of ethyl alcohol. In practice, the actual amount of ethyl alcohol formed is perhaps down by a small percentage as contributions are made to a number of, hopefully beneficial, side reactions. Nevertheless this slight deficiency is allowed for on our wine hydrometer scales and so by using the wine hydrometer correctly, as outlined in a later chapter, it is a simple matter to get a reasonably accurate figure of the total alcohol formed during a complete fermentation merely by direct reading of the hydrometer scale.

FERMENTATION PROGRESS

So far it has been shown that there are two stages of fermentation, but they are not clearly defined and it is often a lack of understanding of these processes which results in so many beginner's failures. The first stage is called the aerobic stage, which merely means that fermentation takes place in the presence of air, and a supply of air dissolved in the must quite apart from that chemically combined in the sugar and the water is absolutely essential in order to build up a vigorous and thriving yeast colony. When water is boiled it will be observed that just before boiling the vessel begins to 'sing' and large bubbles can be seen rising to the surface for some considerable time. This stage is often mistaken for boiling but is, in fact, the point at which the water gives up its dissolved oxygen just before steam appears. This dissolved oxygen is absolutely essential to the colony build-up. What is required for vigorous action inside our fermentation vessel is a whole world of many millions of yeast cells, so that everything being in balance, the process may progress during the following 'anaerobic' stage in which the alcohol is formed.

Many beginners who have not, through lack of knowledge, paid attention to this point and who have boiled their must, or a fair proportion of it, will likely have insufficient air present and hence the colony produced is likely to be under-developed, resulting in a thready and protracted performance which may not completely run its course. Such a fermentation is then said to be 'stuck'.

The very vigorous aerobic stage does not last for very long, maybe just a day or so, and certainly no longer than a few days. Just how long one leaves the must cannot be stated here as this depends on the characteristics of the must and our requirements. Certainly an elderberry pulp should not remain in the must for longer than two and a half to three days, for there is a very real tendency here to extract too much tannin. On the other hand, a cherry must may safely be left on the pulp for seven days or so, and indeed this will be necessary if one is to obtain a reasonable level of colouring.

Because the aerobic stage has begun when carbon dioxide is apparent need not be an immediate cause for concern to get the must completely and safely excluded from air under cover of an airlock, since the rate of carbon dioxide discharge during this time will be so great as to protect the must from airborne contamination anyway. Much depends on how much colouring is required from the pulp and also what fruit pressing facilities are available. If a pulp fermentation is undertaken and only hand pressing in a filter bag is possible, then perhaps a little longer 'on the pulp' may be justified. In such an insurance a slowing of fermentation will likely be experienced due to a lack of sugar, in which case some of the strong sugar solution (SSS) which was made-up at the must preparation stage may be added and stirred in.

Certainly, the must should remain on the pulp no longer than necessary, and when fermentation is really slowing the pulp should be removed and the must transferred to the secondary fermenter without delay and a bung and airlock fitted. The pulp should be

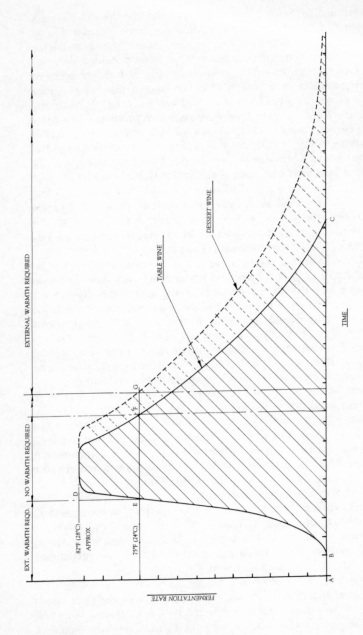

A HYPOTHETICAL INDICATION OF FERMENTATION PROGRESS

EXT. WARMTH REQD. | NO WARMTH REQUIRED | EXTERNAL WARMTH REQUIRED

FERMENTATION RATE

TIME

82°F (28°C) APPROX.

75°F (24°C)

TABLE WINE

DESSERT WINE

strained off via a filter cloth or bag and thoroughly pressed, passing the expressed juice back to the bulk. At this stage it is very useful to be able to take a hydrometer reading, from which you may find that most of the sugar has already been exhausted. In which case, some or all of the remaining strong sugar solution (SSS) should be added. If you are making a table wine which will be of a low alcohol content and will not therefore be pushing the yeast to its limit of tolerance, maybe you will opt to add 50% of this solution, or maybe all of it. Alternatively, if you are making a dessert style you may prefer to add the sugar solution rather more conservatively, so as to encourage the yeast to accept its full operational limits.

But these recommendations are the beginning of what is called 'feeding', which is a method used to push yeasts beyond their normal limits of tolerance and to obtain the maximum possible alcohol content, short of reinforcement with proof spirit. However, with any wine style, when all the sugar is added, the vessel must be kept topped up to within 1 inch (2.5 cm) of the underside of its bung as soon as the reduction in fermentation rate permits.

On the opposite page is a fermentation graph, drawn in an attempt to clarify what has already been said on this subject. But lest any higher mortal takes me to task on the rights or wrongs of this graph, may I hasten to add that it is theoretical only and is produced merely to indicate to the beginner what is likely to be observed throughout the fermentation period. It is not intended to represent any particular readings, quantities or time scales experienced during an actual fermentation. It only takes into account the factors mentioned in this book, and any 'bumps' there should, or should not, be in the curves due to progressive feeding are deliberately omitted.

The vertical component of this graph represents fermentation rate as measured by the evolution of CO_2 and the horizontal component is an expression of time. Point A represents the point or time at which the active starter is introduced into the bulk. It will be seen that for a short period of time, the lag phase, no fermentation is observed. However, an upwards turn of the line begins at Point B after a very short period, which may be in the order of a half to one day or even more, and immediately the rate of fermentation should progressively increase until it reaches a point where the line flattens off horizontally for a short period before turning and sweeping ever more gradually back to the base line where the fermentation rate becomes extinct at point C. Between points D and C is the anaerobic stage, which starts at point D even though the aerobic stage may not have been completed at this point and will go on for a short period, until all the oxygen dissolved in the must is used up.

Now fermentation rate (the vertical ordinate) is another way of saying amount per unit of time — or expressed another way — amount divided by time. And therefore, as the base of the graph represents time, the shaded area under the line must represent the total amount of alcohol produced throughout the fermentation.

The shaded area under the solid line represents the type of curve one may expect for a table wine. Because the yeast is not going to be pushed to its limit, fermentation carries on happily down the slope to point C and ends when the sugar supply is exhausted. This would represent a wine of perhaps some 10 to 12% alcohol by volume.

The additional area bounded by the dotted line is intended to represent the additional amount of alcohol one could reasonably expect to obtain in making a dessert style of wine. Here, because the yeast is being pushed to its limit, the maximum permissible amount of sugar is added before the fermentation rate slows virtually to a standstill, the yeast having completely polluted its own environment. Accordingly, in such a case, the rate of fermentation becomes so slow that the curve tends to disappear off the right hand side of the graph before it reaches the time baseline, and it becomes quite pointless to allow the fermentation to continue. From the graph it can be seen that a very protracted fermentation would add little to the overall area under the curve and therefore very little in the way of additional alcohol.

If fermentation were to stop completely, dropping the curve abruptly back to base, it would indicate that the fermentation had 'stuck' .

SOME COMMENTS ON BATCH SIZE

Something has already been said about batch size in a previous chapter and it may be recalled that recommendation came down heavily in favour of the larger batches of 5 or even 10 (23 or 46 litres) gallons. But these reasons were mainly to do with the logic of reasonable supplies and adequate stocks for correct maturing etc. However, there is another good reason for fermenting in bulk. One of the most important factors for success is that the yeast, and therefore the must itself, be subjected to the temperatures which suit it best. This presents far fewer problems on the larger scale and the reader is urged to take particular note of this fact.

Most of the available commercial wines are produced in climates far warmer than our own; in fact some of them are virtually subtropical. The yeasts we use, which are minute fungi, will operate best in similar conditions. Some authors tell us that temperatures in excess of 100°F (38°C) will kill the yeast and that temperatures below 60°F (16°C) will render it dormant. But, whilst such comments are true, if we deduce from them that 40°F (22°C) is a reasonable working band, we are sadly misled. It is generally accepted for the sake of safety that wine yeasts should not be subjected to temperatures above 75°F (24°C) and I have personally proved this accidentally by experiment. Under the heading 'Principles of Fermentation' in this chapter, it was mentioned that heat is generated whenever one of the two combustible elements combines with oxygen, and it was also shown that when sugar ferments to produce ethyl alcohol, carbon combines with oxygen to form carbon dioxide, and is indeed that which escapes through the airlock. Fermentation produces heat — not very much but it nevertheless warms up the must very slightly until it is slightly warmer than its surroundings, when it can then dissipate this heat. But, if the ambient temperature is too high and the heat cannot escape before the critical temperature of the yeast is reached, fermentation ceases. That temperature, by my own accidental experiment, appears to be in the order of 86°F (30°C). It may vary from one yeast to another but not much.

In my early days of winemaking, it became apparent that too low a temperature was the main reason for my very considerable lack of success. In particular I realized the difficulty of keeping the yeast starter warm and hit on the idea of using a Thermos flask as the starter vessel. I used a Southern Vinyards Vinkwik Yeast, which is known for getting going quite quickly, and as I kept the starter close at hand for observation I fitted the flask with a lightly fitting demijohn cork and airlock so that I could readily observe fermentation and get an idea of its increasing rate. I arranged the starter temperature at 80°F (27°C). After only a couple of hours, CO_2 began to bubble quite strongly from the airlock and I was convinced my starter problems were solved. But after another couple of hours fermentation gradually slowed until it virtually stopped. Following this I left the starter for the remainder of the day and though nothing seemed to happen, an examination of the must indicated it was quite warm. It was, in fact, at a temperature of 86°F (30°C); probably 20°F (11°C) higher than the room temperature. Quite obviously, because the heat generated could not be dissipated through the flask walls, the temperature had gone on increasing until the stalling temperature of the yeast was achieved, and all activity was reduced proportionately to the very low level possible at which the heat could escape which, from a Thermos flask, is very low indeed. When the starter was transferred to a glass bottle fermentation resumed almost immediately.

Another look at the graph on page 62 shows that maximum fermentation rate is achieved at point D, and generally speaking, in our climate, this appears to take place at a temperature of 82°F (28°C). However, if such a high temperature were to persist then the quality of the wine would suffer as volatile esters would be driven off. For practical purposes the winemaker should aim at maintaining a steady temperature not exceeding 75°F (24°C). From what has already been said it will be clear that the rate of fermentation and heat generation is directly proportional and therefore as the fermentation rate increases so also the temperature of the must increases, and a heat generation graph must therefore have a similar form. It will be seen that there is a period, at commencement of fermentation, when external heat needs to be applied (to point E because ambient temperatures are likely to be too low) followed by the peak period when the must is capable of providing its own heat and then, when the quieter period arrives, there is a constantly increasing necessity, starting from point F (or G in the case of a dessert wine), for external heat to be re-applied. Obviously, to be successful, the home winemaker needs to be able to get over this problem and this is very much simpler than one would expect, as will shortly be outlined.

Obviously, the temperature of 82°F (28°C) or thereabouts, is the optimum fermentation point. Lower the must temperature in some way and the fermentation rate would increase until this temperature is once again achieved. Conversely, increase the temperature slightly to approach the stalling temperature of 86°F (30°C) as mentioned above and yeast activity would become suppressed, thereby tending to lower the temperature back to 82°F (28°C). It is for this reason I have shown the fermentation rate to be constant (horizontal) for a short period after point D as both fermentation rate and temperature are obviously maintained constant until such time as the alcohol level increases and the sugar level decreases sufficiently for both temperature and fermentation rate to begin to fall.

So much for the upper temperature tolerated by the yeast. Now what about the lower temperature? Whilst winemakers in general advocate a higher temperature to start fermentation, many recommend a lower temperature be applied as the quiet period sets in. In fact some advocate temperatures as low as 60°F (16°C). Frankly, in my own experience, this is too low and I certainly would not countenance a temperature much below 70°F (21°C). It is claimed that lower temperatures in the latter stages give a better product, but within limits I have not found this to be so, though I am prepared to

66

concede I would not necessarily wish to subject musts to the very maximum temperature throughout the whole fermentation period.

To sum up, the starting temperature is not exceptionally critical, provided sufficient temperature is applied to get the fermentation started. Once this has happened the yeast itself is in control of its own destiny, for a while at any rate, until points F or G are reached on the graph, and by that time a very considerable amount of alcohol will already have been generated. The practical maximum temperature is 75°F (24°C).

Quite apart from the permissible temperature limits advocated here, or for that matter by any other author, yeast does not take kindly to having its temperature shunted back and forth, even within these limits, and it is my firm belief that this factor is the downfall of so many beginners. *The larger a bulk the easier it is to maintain a steady temperature*, and yet beginners are constantly exhorted to make the smaller, one gallon batches with no really satisfactory recommendation as to how temperature may be maintained. The so-called standard 1-gallon (5-litre) fermentation demijohn is very definitely not the ideal vessel in which to ferment and yet its use is almost universal — certainly among beginners.

Apart from the internal heat gains of a fermenting must as already outlined, the only other way temperature can be affected is by gain or loss through the vessel walls. Consider, for a moment, a cubic vessel having sides of 1 centimetre. Because each side has an area of 1 square centimetre and it has six sides, its total surface area is 6 square centimetres. Now consider a vessel having sides of 2 centimetres. Its volume is $2 \times 2 \times 2 = 8$ cubic centimetres, and because each of its six sides has an area of 4 square centimetres it has a total surface area of 24 square centimetres. Compared with the smaller cube its volume is therefore eight times bigger but its surface area is increased only four times. If, therefore, these cubes were to be placed in the same room it follows that the larger cube would heat up or cool down more slowly than the smaller cube when subjected to variations in room temperature. As this feature is true for any shaped volume it follows that a large fermenting vessel will be affected far less by ambient temperature changes than a small one. In fact, commercial wines are made in such large vessels — many thousands of gallons — that their capacity is enormous compared with their surface area; so much so that the warmth generated by the initial vigorous fermentation may well be contained sufficiently long enough for fermentation to be carried through to completion. But the home winemaker is not blessed in this way and we shall shortly be considering ways of overcoming this problem.

One very important factor concerning batch size is the relationship between vessel strength and size for a given shape. Unfortunately, strength varies inversely with increasing size. The larger vessels, particularly the better, glass variety, require far more care in handling than the smaller members of their family. In fact, glass carboys are almost invariably supplied in an outer cradle, usually of plastic these days. When such a vessel is filled, on no account attempt to remove it from its container; should you buy some form of glass vessel not suitably protected, such as that illustrated on page 38, my advice is to make a container, or have one made, before using it.

MAINTAINING WARMTH

Larger batch size has been advocated for the benefit of maintaining a steady temperature during fermentation. In fact, provided fermentation temperature is maintained correctly and steadily, quite small quantities can be made successfully and with confidence. Here again though, the method I personally prefer and therefore advocate lends itself rather better to the larger quantities.

In an American winemaking book I once read, the author recommended three rooms for winemaking, each of some 10 × 8 ft (3.6 × 3.3 metres)! The first was a room with water and washing facilities and having a good sized sink for washing and bottling operations. The second was a fermentation room which I noted with interest he advocated should be maintained at a thermostatically controlled temperature of 75°F (24°C) in order to provide a sustained and satisfactory fermentation. And the third was a padlocked maturing and bottle storage room to hold approximately 1,000 bottles against pilfering hands! This was to be maintained at a steady temperature of 55°F (13°C).

For all three rooms he made further recommendations for lighting etc. and advocated that the fermentation room should also be fitted with extraction fans to carry away the carbon dioxide produced during the process! No doubt he had in mind fermenting perhaps as much as 100 gallons at a time, and in such a case it *would*, perhaps, be prudent to extract this gas as carbon dioxide is a suffocating gas.

However, let us now consider some of the ways of providing and maintaining fermentation warmth, bearing in mind that we should not subject our musts to external temperatures above 75°F (24°C), certainly not below 65°F ($18\frac{1}{2}$°C).

Centrally Heated Home or Rooms

The comfort heat in a centrally heated home is unlikely to be much above 70°F (21°C), in fact the ideal comfort heat for reasonable activity is generally recognized as being 68°F (20°C). It will be seen from what has been said that these figures are, generally speaking, fractionally on the low side for fermentation. These temperatures are most likely to be encountered in the living room, which is the last place most people would wish to see large carboys or a succession of demijohns. Furthermore, heating today is so expensive that such temperatures are rarely maintained continuously — heating levels are generally lowered during the night. In such cases, larger vessels would be better able to contain these fluctuations than the smaller ones, but in either case the overall temperature is really too low.

Other places in the home, such as a spare bedroom, whilst being more acceptable with the family, are likely to be maintained at too low a temperature. To warm a room at all merely to warm a must is both wasteful and unnecessary. And, of course, in the summer, when the central heating is off, rooms can become very cold at night.

If you have a place in the house, maybe near to a central heating boiler, where the temperature is maintained by both day and night within the recommended limits, you are indeed as fortunate as you are rare, and you need consider this important matter no further.

The Airing Cupboard

This is one place frequently used by winemakers, maybe because everyone has one and it is likely to be somewhat warmer than the remainder of the house in general. But the temperature fluctuations in an airing cupboard can be excessive, and are rarely controlled. The chances are that even if you have a good idea of the temperature in your home, you will most likely have little idea of the temperature in your airing cupboard, especially to within 10°F ($5\frac{1}{2}$°C). Furthermore, because it is so small its temperature can change very quickly indeed.

There is too, the marital factor most people need to consider, for a few demijohns of vigorously fermenting elderberry can hardly be regarded as good bedfellows for freshly laundered linen! Frankly, being a lover of peace and concord I have never tried this one, so maybe I prefer to see the drawbacks. Certainly I would never recommend it!

Heated Trays

These are available in a variety of sizes for two, and multiples of two, demijohns up to about ten. They are often sold to beginners because of their simplicity, but like many simple things, they do have a quite serious drawback in use which can only result in complications, as many will have encountered. The big disadvantage is that in general they are not thermostatically controlled. The trays are electrically heated internally, and usually have plastic surfaces with small rubber feet on the underside.

To maintain the temperature of a fermenting must needs external heat *after* the vigorous period when the sugar quantity is dwindling and when the vigour of the yeast is also declining due to the inhibiting effect of the ever-mounting alcohol content. In these circumstances, the yeast tends to fall out of suspension, dropping to the bottom of the vessel, and the characteristics of the tray are such that, in an effort to maintain the correct overall temperature of the must, its surface needs to be considerably warmer than the yeast can accept. Hence, the yeast falls to the position where the heat is greatest and is often killed.

Of course, one may be able to control this adverse characteristic by arranging a small air gap between tray and vessel and ensuring that the tray is not stood on carpet when it may become very hot indeed, but I regard such resorts to be highly unsatisfactory. There are too many uncontrolled outside influences which can have adverse effects on the desired result.

Heated Bands or Belts

There is a good variety of these on the market. They are made to slip over the outer diameter of the fermentation vessel, and are supplied in a range of electrical capacities and physical sizes to suit most vessels. Many are thermostatically controlled.

Thermostatically Controlled Immersion Heaters

This method of maintaining warmth is my favourite, offering what is technically a most superior and yet inexpensive solution to the all-important matter of maintaining fermentation warmth.

This method is the only one in which the heater and its control equipment are fully immersed in the liquid whose temperature is to be controlled. One is not getting heat from somewhere else and hoping that it is not too little or too much. Certainly, my early winemaking days were dogged with repeated stuck fermentations, even when using commercially prepared concentrates, and I can honestly say that since using a heater of this type I have not experienced another. This *must* be good news for many a failed beginner.

Immersion heaters are designed in the form of a tube of heat-resisting glass and look rather like a very large test tube. They are sealed off at the top end by a watertight rubber bung, through which the electrical cable is bonded. The heating element is invariably in the lower part of the tube with the thermostatic control equipment immediately above. Hence, whilst it is usually permissible for some part of the top of the heater to protrude from the must, especially in the early stages of fermentation when the total volume of water may not have been added, the heater controls function best when virtually fully submerged so that the controller is able to sense the liquid temperature rather than that of the air immediately above.

The physical sizes vary somewhat from make to make, and range in electrical capacity from about 50 to 120 watts. Naturally, the smaller powered ones have sufficient power for use with the smaller sized vessels and these tend to be somewhat smaller in physical size for this reason. Some of the smaller ones incorporate a rubber bung at the top end which is extended to fit a demijohn neck, but this tends to restrict their use.

The best heater combines the smallest physical size with the highest electrical capacity or heat output. A 100 watt heater is certainly capable of maintaing the warmth of a 10-gallon (46-litre) brew, particularly if the container is insulated in some way, perhaps with an old blanket or car rug. Always opt for the higher power if the heater is intended for use with a range of sizes of vessel, because the thermostat will ensure that the set temperature is maintained regardless of electrical rating. The higher power will just mean that the heater is automatically switched on by the thermostat for shorter periods. Low powered heaters may have insufficient capacity to maintain the warmth of a large brew. In such a case the set temperature would never be achieved and the heater would remain on continually.

The set temperature of a heater is usually 75°F (24°C), which is wholly satisfactory for general use, and the temperature of some heaters can be adjusted up or down by a few degrees should the operator so wish.

Now for the methods of use. Earlier, recommendations were made to carry out primary fermentation in a winemaking bucket because this is more convenient, both in containing the vigorous stage of fermentation and in the handling of pulp etc., and then to continue the quieter anaerobic stage in a glass vessel and under the protection of an airlock. Clearly then, both vessels must be adapted in some way to incorporate use of the immersion heater.

With the bucket, it is necessary to have an accurately sized hole in the lid to accommodate a large rubber bung, preferably the same bung as that to be used in the secondary glass fermenter. The bung must be bored to receive a large sized airlock and a somewhat smaller hole will be necessary for passage of the heater cable. The hole in the bucket lid must be cut very accurately because it is essential that the bung is airtight when fitted, otherwise the airlock will not work and harmful micro-organisms which could destroy the wine will be free to enter. It is a good plan to draw a circle very carefully on the lid around the small end of the bung and then to ensure that the hole is made no larger. It can be cut out very easily with a Stanley knife or similar, and then trimmed to size very carefully, finishing off with a small, sharp file. If you are not very good at this sort of thing then get someone else to do it for you. It is possible to buy fermentation buckets with a hole provided in the container to hold a bung. When this particular feature is not required, the bucket and lid can be used with a plain, unbored bung fitted. The arrangement described can be seen in figure one below, and in the illustrations on pages 38 and 40.

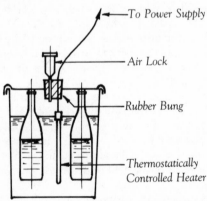

Fig. 1
Primary Fermenter
(with Starter Bottles)

Alternatively, if you do not wish to cut the bucket lid, another method is to cut a short length of $\frac{1}{4}$ inch (6 mm) diameter wood dowelling so that it fits diagonally across the bucket to form a support bar as shown below, figure two. Next, fit two small elastic bands to the bar as spacers and then, with two more elastic bands, attach the heater to the bar. Arrange the elastic bands towards the upper end of the glass cylinder so that they are not in contact with the glass immediately adjacent to the heating element. Finally place the bar in the bucket ensuring that the heater is securely held and that it is not touching the bottom or walls of the bucket. Do not use anything as a support bar that is likely to taint the fermentation in any way. If small diameter dowelling is not available, use a piece of glass syphon tube or rod accurately cut to length. Some manufacturers supply their heaters with special clips, usually fitted with suckers intended to adhere to the bucket wall.

The electric cable will need to pass over the rim of the bucket, but it should be found that this will not prevent the lid from being 'snapped' into position. In fact, the very small air gap created by the cable between the bucket and lid is necessary to permit escape of the carbon dioxide gas discharge during the vigorous stage. Otherwise the bucket may become severely pressurized. Again, wrap the bucket to lessen heat loss.

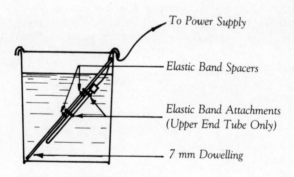

To Power Supply

Elastic Band Spacers

Elastic Band Attachments
(Upper End Tube Only)

7 mm Dowelling

Fig. 2
Primary Fermenter
(Alternative Heating Arrangement)

Earlier in this chapter the various problems of maintaining warmth were discussed. Clearly then, as a heater for a starter bottle would be impracticable, and yet bearing in mind its great need for warmth because it is so small, some provision has to be made. Accordingly, in figure one opposite, a method of maintaining starter bottle warmth is shown. Up to half a dozen starter bottles can be kept right on temperature in this way, using just one heater. Make up the starter bottle or bottles exactly as outlined on page 57 and adjust the water content slightly; do not worry if the bottles tend to float, they certainly will not tip over and will be held down when the lid is snapped into place. The level of the heating water or must should not be too high but should be sufficient to cover the heater satisfactorily. If the must has been used as the heating medium, it will, of course, be at the correct temperature when the time comes to introduce the starter into it.

As starter bottles really need to get off to a good start, and therefore require the correct temperature, they often tend to 'blow their top' and become very messy in the process. However, any overflow with this method merely discharges into the heating water or must. In fact, as the starter or starters are enclosed within the bucket, there is no need for a cotton wool plug in the bottle neck(s).

Sometimes it is difficult to get the heater cable to pass through the hole in the bung and if the hole is bored too large it is often not airtight, as the cable is usually of an oval section. However, passage of the cable can be assisted by smearing a little soap or washing-up liquid over the cable during threading. Conversely, if the hole is not really airtight, a little vaseline (not car grease) may be applied around the top of the hole. If the airlock pulses properly during fermentation, then it can be assumed that there are no unwanted air leaks.

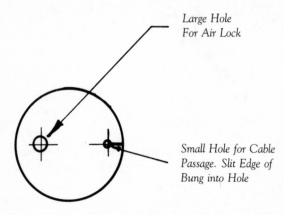

Large Hole
For Air Lock

Small Hole for Cable
Passage. Slit Edge of
Bung into Hole

Fig. 3
Rubber Bung
(As Fitted to Fig. 1, p. 72)

To overcome these problems bore the cable hole very near to the edge of the bung, a little on the small side. The wall of the bung is then cut through into the hole from top to bottom as shown in figure three opposite, using a straightedge and very sharp cutter. The hole, being near to the edge allows some additional flexibility which is usually sufficient to permit a seal when the bung is pressed home. It also allows the cable to be fitted and removed without removing the power plug and permits easy movement of the bung on the cable to suit varying sizes of vessel and to facilitate thorough cleaning.

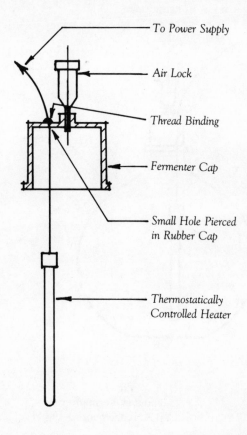

To Power Supply

Air Lock

Thread Binding

Fermenter Cap

Small Hole Pierced
in Rubber Cap

Thermostatically
Controlled Heater

Fig. 4
Fermenter Cap

75

Instead of a bung, some glass vessels are now being supplied with a tightly over-fitting rubber or plastic cap designed to receive an airlock. With these it is quite satisfactory to make a small hole in the rubber, as shown in figure four, page 75, with the point of a sharp pair of scissors. When the cable is passed through, it is airtight and the position of the heater can be arranged by binding the cable with thread when the cap is in the desired position. If such a cap is used instead of a bung in conjunction with a fermenter, as shown in figure five below, it can be slid out of the way along the cable easily allowing the rubber bung to be fitted as an alternative or when used in the bucket lid as in figure one.

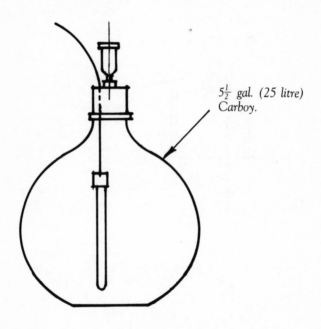

$5\frac{1}{2}$ gal. (25 litre) Carboy.

Fig. 5
Secondary Fermenter
(With Cap Arrangement as Fig. 4)

Please note that these immersion heaters are very similar in specification to those supplied for maintaining warmth in a fish tank. However, fish tank heaters usually have metal parts and therefore must not be used for winemaking, otherwise your finished product may well be completely ruined through metal contamination.

Heated Cupboards

To make one, or a variety of small batches of wine at any particular time employing a number of demijohns, this can be done quite satisfactorily in a heated cupboard. An old kitchen wall cabinet of the standard 40-inch (1-metre) wide size can be readily adapted to house five demijohns by lowering its shelf to within a few inches of the bottom and by fitting a couple of batten-type lampholders in the small space below. The lampholders should be fitted to the sides of the cabinet and *not* the bottom as any spillage must not come into contact with the electrical wiring.

An old cabinet of this type can be satisfactorily mounted on a garage or outhouse wall; two 60 watt lamps operated through a simple, room-type thermostat mounted in the cabinet should provide all the warmth necessary to maintain a temperature within the fermentation vessels, even in the coldest weather. In fact, one such lamp should maintain the temperature but two are recommended so that should one blow, fermentation will not be adversely affected until such time as a replacement lamp is fitted. If a thermostat is not fitted, lower powered lamps may be used — try 15 or 25 watts. Since warmed air rises it will be necessary to pay some attention to door sealing, particularly at the top, possibly by using ordinary self-adhesive sponge draught excluder. It is also important to ensure that heat rising from the lamps is not directed on to the underside of the shelf immediately below a demijohn, to eliminate the danger of the yeast at the base being heated above its tolerance level. If such an arrangement cannot be avoided then some form of heat deflector immediately above the bulbs will be necessary.

A couple of words of warning, though. When such a cabinet is brought into use, it is advisable to check its performance initially over a period of hours using demijohns filled with water. It is necessary to ensure that the liquid temperature is maintained at 75°F (24°C) or thereabouts, regardless of the thermostat setting, for it will be appreciated that this method of temperature control cannot possibly be so good as that achieved by immersion heaters as the control equipment is merely sensing the air temperature in its vicinity rather than that of the liquid itself. As hot air rises, the chamber is likely to be quite a few degrees hotter at the top than the bottom.

POWER PLUG

L = LIVE (BROWN)
N = NEUTRAL (BLUE)
E = EARTH (GREEN/YELLOW)

THERMOSTAT

LAMP

LAMP

ARRANGE CABLE ENTRY THROUGH
BACK PANEL. POSITON ALL
WIRING INSIDE LAMPHOUSE TO
PROTECT FROM SPILLAGE ETC.

WIRING DIAGRAM FOR DOMESTIC
HEATING TYPE THERMOSTAT

ONE 5½ GALL. (25L) BUCKET
SHOWN IN THIS VIEW

END VIEW
(CUT THROUGH CENTRE)

2 60 WATT LAMP'S
(SEE WIRING DIAG)

ONE 5 GALL (23L) CARBOY
SHOWN IN THIS VIEW

MATERIAL LIST:
1 BASEBOARD — 22" × 18" × ⅝" THICK BLOCKBOARD
(56cm × 46cm × 16mm)
2 BACKBOARD — 22" × 18" × ⅝" THICK BLOCKBOARD
(56cm × 46cm × 16mm)
3 FRONT BAFFLE — 22" × 18" × ⅝" THICK BLOCKBOARD
(56cm × 46cm × 16mm)
4 LAMPHOUSE COVER — 22" × 5" × 3/16" THICK PLYWOOD
(56cm × 12cm × 5mm)
5 END PANELS (2) — 18" × 18⅝" × 3/16" THICK PLYWOOD
(46cm × 47cm × 5mm)
6 SPILLAGE RAIL — 22" × ¾" × ¼" HARDWOOD
(56cm × 20mm × 6mm)
7 BASEBOARD MOUNTINGS (2) — 18" × ¾" × ¼" HARDWOOD
(46cm × 20mm × 6mm)
8 BATTEN TYPE STANDARD LAMPHOLDERS (2)
9 DOMESTIC HEATING THERMOSTAT

8 1" (2.5CM) DIA. HOLES
IN FRONT BAFFLE.
POSITION AS SHOWN

1½"

7½"

7½"

1½"

1½"

FRONT VIEW

10"
CRS.

PLAN

5 DEMIJOHNS SHOWN
IN THIS VIEW

2"

SCREWED CONSTRUCTION THROUGHOUT

ARRANGEMENT OF TEMPERATURE CONTROLLED FERMENTER HEATER

(SEE TEXT)

Lastly, a wall-mounted cupboard housing five demijohns is very heavy indeed and it will be necessary to ensure that the mounting brackets are very firmly fixed to both the cabinet and the wall. An extra insurance would be to mount a couple of shelf brackets immediately below the cabinet so as to accept some of the weight. Certainly, mounting on coke breeze or expanded concrete insulation blocks must be avoided.

A better alternative to the heated cupboard, but working on the same principle, is a heater such as that shown in the drawing on the opposite page, and if you have some wood, good quality chipboard or blockboard handy, one can be made in just a few hours. The finished size of each component is given on the drawing, so if you prefer, you could have these ready cut to size by a timber merchant and merely screw them together yourself. The heating arrangement is basically the same as that described above and a wiring diagram to suit both is given on the drawing.

An attempt has been made here to obviate some of the difficulties which can be experienced with the heated cupboard and the sizes shown make the arrangement a lot more versatile. For instance, the baseboard has been sized to house five demijohns, one $5\frac{1}{2}$-gallon (25-litre) fermentation bucket or one 5-gallon (23-litre) carboy in its cradle, so that any production method decided upon can be accommodated. It will be noticed that the bulbs are mounted behind the platform so that the considerable heat immediately rising from them is not directed onto the must. The air openings and baffle-board are arranged to ensure that the warmed air is circulated over and around the fermentation vessel or vessels and the position of the lamps and baffle-board ensure that all wiring is safe from any spillage or vigorous overflow.

The method of operation here is to stand the heater on a table or garage bench and, having positioned the fermentation vessel or vessels, carefully cover the whole arrangement with a couple of layers of old blanket or car rug so that the vessel or vessels are completely enclosed.

Studying the drawing opposite, it will be seen that the baffle-board has two large holes bored in it at a low level, immediately in front of the bulbs, so that cooled air will be induced over the bulb envelopes. There are two further holes at mid-height at either end of the baffle-board, through which the warmed air is returned to the fermentation section. For air circulation these holes must be higher than the two at the base of the bulbs, but they should not be at the top of the baffle-board because the warmed air must be introduced back into the fermentation section at as low a level as possible.

Remember, hot air rises and it needs to rise and circulate in the fermentation section, not the lamp compartment. In this way heat loss through the cover is minimized.

The sort of thermostat advocated for use here and for the wall cupboard is of the type used for space heating control in a domestic central heating system but not, of course, incorporating a time clock. These are quite cheap and are of the simple ON/OFF type.

For safety, it is important that the fermenter is made and wired correctly. Do not use with bulbs exposed or use bulbs of a higher power than specified; and use only a non-flammable cover such as a wool blanket.

Should it be thought desirable to insulate either of the heaters advocated, it may be done very cheaply by purchasing a few large-sized expanded polystyrene ceiling tiles. These can be cut with a sharp knife and cemented in position on the walls using the appropriate adhesive. But do not use in close proximity to the lamps.

STUCK FERMENTATIONS

Sticking is a condition in which fermentation slows and ultimately stops before it should, so that the intended alcohol level is not achieved and a proportion of the sugar remains unfermented, rendering the wine sweeter than required. If the fermentation slows and stops at a very early stage it may be possible to re-vitalize it satisfactorily once the cause has been removed. But if sticking happens towards the end of the fermentation it may not be possible to re-start the activity. In this case, disappointment is almost inevitable, for if fermentation ceases with a specific gravity above 1025, the wine will be too sweet even for what is generally accepted as a sweet wine. Even if below this figure, should the wine have been of the dry table variety with an anticipated alcohol range in the order of 10 to 12%, then the lower alcohol level combined with the additional sweetness will result in a very disappointing, unstable concoction.

Listed below are the generally accepted causes of sticking:

1) Acid imbalance	5) Dissolved oxygen deficiency
2) Must imbalance	6) High level of sterilants
3) Nutrient deficiency	7) Excess sugar
4) Under-developed yeast colony	8) Excess alcohol
	9) Incorrect temperature

Most of these items have been dealt with at length elsewhere. Excess

80

alcohol applies to table wines and occurs, of course, when too much sugar has been added to the must. As the alcohol level in a must increases so the yeast becomes less able to perform its task, as it is poisoning its own environment. If the must and the starter have been prepared correctly the yeast colony grows very quickly to consume what has been provided for its sustenance, but in so doing, its environment finally brings it to a standstill. The aim of the winemaker who seeks high alcohol levels must be to maintain the ideal environment for the yeast and to gradually bring the yeast up to its maximum alcohol tolerance level.

Often, though, beginners feed their must with too much sugar, particularly in the latter stages of making a dessert style wine, with the result that fermentation ceases before all the sugar can be converted. In such a case it may also be necessary to re-adjust the acid level slightly to bring it up to a value which will restore the imbalance exerted by the excess sugar. If, however, the gravity is too high, there is little that can be done, except perhaps to blend it with a similar but drier wine.

It is for the reasons outlined that sticking is more troublesome when it occurs towards the latter end of fermentation. The only way to deal with a problem of this sort, once having established and rectified the cause, is to employ what is known as the doubling-up process. A new, active, starter is prepared and put into a vessel with 1 pint (570 ml) of the stuck must. When this is actively fermenting again, a further pint (570 ml) is added. When this quantity is positively active it is doubled by adding a further 2 pints (1.14 litres) and so on until all of the stuck must is active again. But this is not as simple as it sounds. In fact it is fraught with problems, not the least of which is maintaining correct temperature whilst these small, abnormal quantities are being handled.

This is the most common cause of sticking, particularly for beginners. Certainly my own stuck fermentations were all, without exception, attributable to this cause and since operating as outlined in this and preceding chapters, stuck fermentations have, for me, become a thing of the past. I know of numerous beginners who have suffered the most disappointing and off-putting failures and I am certain that in most cases incorrect temperature — usually a lack of it — has been at the root of their problem. And this is why I have paid very considerable attention to this feature in this chapter. It is in the very latest stages of fermentation that risks with temperature should not be taken, for it is stuck fermentations which occur at this point which can prove to be so disastrous. In my experience the improvements to be gained by lowering temperatures at the latter stages are marginal indeed. Surely, if one is in search of perfection, the risk of even the slightest degree of sticking should be out of the question.

SUMMING UP

1. Always use a vigorously active yeast starter to initiate fermentation.
2. Choose a yeast suitable for the intended wine style and do not skimp on this item.
3. Always ensure that your starters and musts are maintained within the correct temperature range.
4. Where possible, carry out initial fermentation (aerobic stage) in a fermentation bucket having a close-fitting lid.
5. Always carry out the secondary fermentation (anaerobic stage) in a closed fermenter fitted with an airlock.
6. Do not allow pulp fermentations to remain on the pulp for any longer then necessary, especially fruit known to be high in tannin.
7. Make the largest batch size you can reasonably handle.
8. Do not use boiled or boiling water in musts. Boiling large quantities in a domestic kitchen is a dangerous practice.
9. Handle large-sized glass fermenters with great care.
10. Avoid stuck musts at all costs.

CHAPTER 8

CLARIFICATION AND BULK STORAGE

This is the next step following fermentation, although in most cases clarification begins some time before fermentation ceases and by this time is often well advanced. Clarification is the stage at which the cloudiness which characterizes a fermenting wine clears, or is made to clear, and the unwanted debris in suspension gravitates to the bottom of the vessel. However, because this debris invariably stems from a number of causes it may be necessary to tread a few well-used steps during the bulk storage stage in order to remove it all before bottling.

It is true to say that most wines will clear of their own accord eventually but some may take a very long time indeed and, by all practical definitions, a few may never clear at all. Such wines require our special attention and the main remedies in simplified and practical form are discussed in this chapter. Certainly, clarification is a very important part of winemaking, for no-one is likely to truthfully enthuse over a glass of wine which is not star bright. Not only will the visible delight of clarity be missing but also the all important taste and bouquet are likely to be adversely affected too, by the presence of unwanted and unpalatable inclusions. This is the stage therefore which will demonstrate your real winemaking knowledge and ability.

RACKING AND SULPHITING

This is the first activity following fermentation and is the operation *always* undertaken following production of a batch of wine, unlike those activities to be described later, which in some cases will not be necessary. It is the action of syphoning the newly made wine from one vessel to another, thus separating it from the yeast debris which, at that stage, is already collecting at the bottom of the fermentation vessel. Certainly, towards the end of fermentation a quite considerable layer of sediment will have fallen out of suspension as fermentation slows and there is no longer a really positive upsurge of carbon dioxide bubbles to keep the contents really active.

The first of a number of rackings should take place no more than a few days after fermentation ceases, which is clearly apparent because carbon dioxide bubbles cease to pass through the airlock. In this way most of the debris, or lees as it is normally called, will be removed at a very early stage before it can autolyse — self-induced destruction — and break down to create off-flavours in the finished wine. At this stage, too, the newly racked wine should be dosed with 1 teaspoon (5 ml) of 10% stock campden solution per gallon (5 litres) (see Chapter Four) or, one campden tablet should be crushed and thoroughly dissolved for each gallon (5 litres). The adding of campden at this stage is very important as it will prevent oxidation killing off bacteria and any remaining yeast which may otherwise still be active, thereby encouraging it to settle in readiness for further rackings in due course.

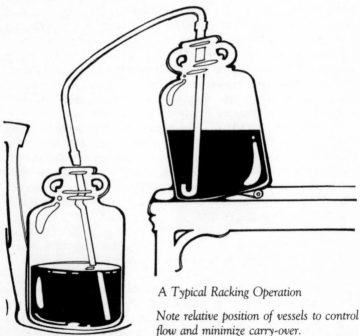

A Typical Racking Operation

Note relative position of vessels to control flow and minimize carry-over.

Subsequently, the wine should be racked twice more, at three to four month intervals or when any significant level of lees has formed. At these further two rackings roughly half of the above quantity of campden solution should be added each time but no further doses should be added if yet more rackings are undertaken. Care must be taken not to build the sulphite level too high as it will persist in the finished wine giving an off-flavour that will take months to disperse. Each time the wine is racked a small quantity will be lost and it will therefore be necessary to make up the deficiency in the storage vessel to within about 1 inch (2.5 cm) of the closure, either with a similar wine or a little water. The illustration on the page opposite shows how a wine should be racked from one vessel to another to remove it from the lees. Whether 1-gallon (5-litre) demijohns are used or larger vessels will depend entirely upon the scale of your operations, but the principle shown remains the same. In order to prevent spillage make sure that the lower vessel is at least as big as the upper one. Preferably it should be the same size for if it is larger you will need to pass the wine back to the initial vessel, first having thoroughly washed it.

Apart from the additional vessel you will see that a length of plastic tubing is used, together with a glass or rigid plastic syphon tube as shown on page 29. It will now be appreciated why the end of this tube is turned upwards so as to minimize any entrainment of the lees during racking. But do not worry if a little is carried over, it will settle out and be removed quite successfully at subsequent rackings. To start the process, the vessels should be placed in their relative positions, as shown, taking care in handling the upper vessel so as not to disturb the lees. Needless to say, the transfer vessel should be thoroughly washed and sterilized before use. It then remains to attach the flexible plastic tube to the syphon tube and, inserting the syphon tube carefully into the wine, the far end of the flexible tube is placed in the mouth and sucked. When sufficient wine has been drawn up, the end should be quickly transferred to the lower vessel and pushed to the bottom so that it is submerged as quickly as possible as transfer commences.

This technique may take a little practice, for if insufficient wine is drawn up, transfer will not commence. On the other hand, wine should *not* be drawn up into the mouth as this may develop into an undesirable habit with a resulting need for excessive topping-up! Make sure that the inlet end, that is the part in the original vessel, is submerged continuously, gradually lowering it as necessary to the final position illustrated. In this way the transfer of liquid performed efficiently will leave little but lees in the upper vessel.

Flow will be maintained by the liquid travelling from a high level to a low. Hence the rate of flow will lessen as the level in the upper vessel drops and that of the lower vessel correspondingly rises. The arrangement shown on page 84 is most convenient as the rate of flow will be least towards the end of transfer when the two surfaces approach the same level thus minimizing the possibility of entrainment of the lees at the point when this is most likely to occur.

When racking is completed, and the vessel topped up, it must be provided with a suitable closure such as a cork and put on one side for commencement of bulk storage.

Pectin Test

Should a pectin haze be suspected at this stage and, if pectolytic enzyme was not used or perhaps it was added when the must was too warm, a sample test should be made. Take about 3 teaspoons (15 ml) of methylated spirit and add 1 teaspoon (5 ml) of the wine. If pectin is present this procedure causes it to 'gel' and small blobs or jelly like clots can be seen forming in the solution. However, these do not form immediately and it may be necessary to wait a couple of hours or so. If the presence of pectin is confirmed, pectolytic enzyme should be added according to the manufacturer's instructions in the hope that the wine will subsequently clear, but addition at this stage is really no substitute for adding it at the preparation stage of the must.

Starch Test

The standard test for the presence of starch if it is suspected is the iodine test. Take about one teaspoon (5 ml) of the wine and add it to a few drops of iodine solution, which can be purchased quite cheaply from any chemist. If the solution turns distinctly blue–black then starch is present. This must not, however, be mistaken for the brownish shade imparted to the solution by the iodine itself. If starch is present amylase should now be added.

PROTEIN HAZES AND FININGS

Sub-microscopic particles which make up persistent hazes are generally protein and are colloidal in nature, carrying a minute electrical charge. Like all electrical charges they can be positive or negative but the presence of a colloid in our wine is likely to be positive.

As is well known, the positive and negative or North and South poles of a magnet have a great attraction for one another whilst 'like' poles, either North or South, repel. Quite obviously, then, the sub-microscopic protein particles will be of a like nature and will repel each other, thereby trying to create the greatest distance between themselves according to the strength of their electrical field. But because there are so many of these particles within the confines of the liquid, they can only push themselves as far apart as possible before coming under the influence of the repelling field of other particles in their vicinity. They are therefore held in colloidal suspension throughout the wine and can remain so indefinitely.

In these instances it becomes necessary to introduce into the wine particles of opposing polarity, causing them to attract those already present and thereby neutralizing both their respective electrical fields; they will then agglomerate and fall out of suspension. As has already been said, the particles constituting a wine haze are likely to be positive, and it is therefore necessary to introduce a substance containing negative particles. One such substance is called Bentonite.

Bentonite is a natural montmorillonite clay obtained from various parts of the world and takes its name from Fort Benton in Wyoming, USA, an area from whence it was originally obtained. It has to be made up into a suspension in water and at first appears to be reluctant to do so. But it should be prepared in the quantity and strength recommended according to the manufacturers' instructions for the quantity of wine requiring treatment, perhaps encouraging it through a fine kitchen sieve during mixing and keeping the solution well agitated for a good period before introduction and thorough dispersal in the bulk. The bulk should subsequently be agitated regularly over the following few days and then left to settle, after which it should be carefully racked in the manner already described.

A considerable latitude regarding the amount of Bentonite suspension to be added to the bulk of wine is possible but because the negative particles attract and neutralize the positive particles in the wine, it is clearly possible to add too much, leaving yet another haze of predominantly negative particles.

Very occasionally, Bentonite will not clear a wine and then the last practical recourse for the home winemaker is use of a wine fining gel. These are normally based on isinglass, which is a preparation from the swim bladder of the sturgeon fish. It is as well to remember that a fining of this type may cause a deficiency of tannin in the wine. If there is clearly a lack of astringency following fining, some extra tannin should be added.

Numerous fining agents have been used over the years, including egg white, milk, casein, gelatine and ox blood, but these are no longer used by the home winemaker, for even the apparently simple use of egg white is most inconvenient due to the very small quantity required for use in home wine batches.

METALLIC HAZES

A metallic haze is a haze due to metal entering into solution at some time during the winemaking process. They must never be tolerated and are certainly unlikely to occur if only the equipment and advice on materials of construction advocated in Chapter Five are observed. Certainly, contact with tin, copper, zinc, iron or lead is capable of tainting your wines and they are very dangerous to health. Any items containing lead, particularly certain old fashioned vessels having a relatively soft lead-glazed surface and occasionally used in the past for fermenting, must be ruthlessly avoided. If in doubt about any vessel or equipment, do not use it. Lead is highly toxic and, absorbed into the system, has a cumulative effect resulting in serious illness. Wherever the presence of metal is suspected the wine must be ruthlessly discarded.

BULK STORAGE

Bulk storage is, of course, the primary part of the maturation process, a process which continues after bottling. It would be virtually impossible to outline all that goes on during the ageing process, but it is a very important period nevertheless. Newly fermented wine is rough and sometimes downright unpleasant, for it can both taste and smell of yeast and other impurities. It lacks the flavour, roundness and balance which can only come in the fullness of time. Just how much time is really quite impossible to assess, for it depends on so many factors, but certainly some characteristics are better formed at this stage whilst others occur after bottling. Red wines require more time than white and the strong dessert variety more than table wines. The ageing rate also varies according to the storage conditions and vessels used. But, nevertheless, during this period there will be a slow degree of oxidation bringing gradual and beneficial changes.

During the fermentation period the primary intention is to produce alcohol and, regardless of what some novices may think, the alcohol level will in no way increase once fermentation is completed and maturation commences. No amount of maturing strengthens wines, it will only improve the taste and aroma. In addition to alcohol, fermentation produces acids and 'in between' substances called aldehydes. Alcohol and acids combine on a very small scale to form esters; esters provide much of the aroma and flavour, and it is at this stage that the oiliness appears which creates the characteristic 'curtains' on a wine glass during consumption. Some of these esters also originate from the fruit itself and this is a further reason why no ingredients should be boiled or even excessively heated at the preparation stage. Malic acid, found in apples, is particularly important in ester formation — see under malic acid, page 52 — and this is why at least a little malic acid is a useful addition to any must.

The best ageing temperature range is in the order to 50° to 60°F (10 to $15\frac{1}{2}$°C) as this is the temperature at which the maturing rate will be as reasonably quick as possible whilst allowing no possibility of fermentation recommencing. Too high a temperature accelerates the oxidation rate unduly, causing darkening and a flatness of taste. On other hand, too low a temperature slows everything down.

The oxidation rate is fastest in wooden casks, but the batches produced by the home winemaker, even when operating on a reasonable scale, are far too small for satisfactory maturing in such vessels. Keep to glass, as sufficient oxygen will have been absorbed into the bulk during the racking sessions immediately preceding this stage. In fact, when increasing the scale of production, the demijohns formerly used for fermentation make very good maturing vessels. Corks must be used and not rubber bungs, as the former tend to permit a reasonable quantity of air to enter. The vessels should be topped up to within an inch (25 mm) of the underside of the cork.

Maturation should be undertaken in a darkened place and at least out of the way of direct sunlight. The corner of a garage for this purpose can be very useful as many do not even have a window but some thought must be given to the temperature which can fluctuate quite considerably.

FILTERS & FILTRATION

Filtering and filtration form a very important part of the clarification process. Filtration should be considered as being the last step in the clarification process and certainly nor the first. In the methods of clarification discussed so far, none have involved the setting up of a physical barrier through which a wine is passed and upon which unwanted particles may be arrested. But certainly, because filters employ this seemingly positive method one should not make the mistake of regarding a filter as being the 'ultimate weapon' and that, provided a filter is available, the clarification methods already discussed can be ignored. It is indeed true to say that, following a number of rackings, a wine may well fall clear, especially when given a reasonable period of bulk storage, and neither finings nor filtration may be necessary. Accordingly a need for filtration may only become apparent following a considerable period of bulk storage, often immediately preceding bottling.

There are one or two characteristics and limitations which need to be observed in order to make the best use of filters and, of course, there are various types available to the amateur, some showing distinct advantages over others. For instance it is a characteristic of filters that the finer they filter, the less filtering will be done before the filter medium becomes blocked, or blinded as it is sometimes called. Accordingly, it would be quite problematic to attempt to treat a wine having a very heavy sediment of what are relatively large particles. In such a case a filter may well become blinded three or four times when filtering merely 1 gallon (5 litres), and clearly this is not acceptable. Once a filter has been set up it should be quite capable of clearing at least 5 gallons (23 litres) of wine, and maybe even 10 or 20 gallons (46 or 92 litres).

Conversely, although a haze may appear to be quite murky, it may nevertheless be colloidal in nature being made up of particles so small as to pass through the filter as though it were not there. The filtered wine will then appear as clouded as hitherto. The two different types of haze are indistinguishable to the naked eye.

Bearing these factors in mind it becomes clear that solid particles in a wine must not be so numerous as to block the filter, nor so small (even if they *are* numerous) as to pass straight through it. Fortunately the particles normally arrested by a filter are not colloidal in nature and filters and finings are complementary to each other, but filters alone cannot take the place of finings. Also, a lot of the material arrested by a filter would clearly fall out of suspension given sufficient bulk storage time.

Filters are often criticized for taking something out of a wine, or bestowing a 'cardboard' taste. If the use of filters were to have an adverse effect, then certainly they would not be so universally used as they are commercially. And amateurs entering competitions would not resort to filtering either, as prizes are won on taste and bouquet as well as clarity!

Undoubtedly, the underlying problem facing amateurs is the fact that they subject the wine to excessive doses of atmospheric air and thus oxygen, which can very easily lead to oxidation. This condition is sometimes referred to as filtration sickness and though a wine may recover in time a severe case may well cause irreparable damage.

This same condition can happen also during bottling when it is referred to as bottle sickness. This is another good reason why filtration should be left to a time immediately preceding bottling so that it is subjected to one dosage of air rather than two. And, very importantly, it is highly desirable to sulphite the wine *before* filtering rather than immediately prior to bottling.

The elaborate and expensive filters used commercially in wine production do not subject the product to air in the same way, indeed professionally the filter may be fed with an inert gas such as nitrogen or carbon dioxide so that no oxidation can take place. Commercial producers are all too aware of the importance of marketing a product which is star bright. The amateur too must also have this awareness.

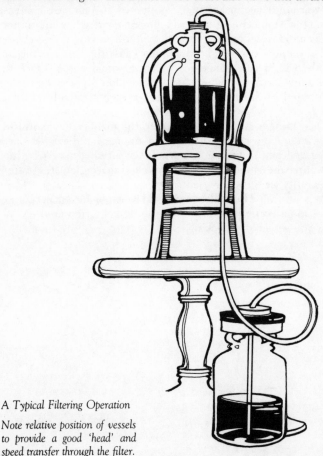

A *Typical Filtering Operation*

Note relative position of vessels to provide a good 'head' and speed transfer through the filter.

Most filters work on the gravity principle and a typical filtering set-up is shown on page 91. In order to speed filtration as much as possible, the distance between the upper and lower vessels is exaggerated compared with the illustration on page 84 showing the racking process. The additional height increases the static head. Because of the physical barrier presented by the filtering medium, gravity filtering is very much slower than racking and tends to slow even more as the filter becomes contaminated. Thus the more 'head' one can obtain the better, but do not try to lift large, heavy vessels unassisted. It is far better to lessen the 'head' and wait a little longer than to chance a mishap in which you could lose your brew and equipment or worse, injure yourself.

If you are a beermaker or feel disposed to purchase a carbon dioxide (CO_2) injector, it is possible to remove much of the air from the receiving vessel before starting to filter by giving it a good blow out, but do not do anything which may cause the vessel to pressurize, otherwise a very dangerous situation would ensue. Once the vessel is filled with carbon dioxide and the filter is placed on the top as illustrated it will remain in the vessel, as carbon dioxide is heavier than air.

When using a filter, always observe the manufacturer's instructions. Thoroughly wetting the filter will ensure that the outlet side is washed and free from minute particles of filtering material which could otherwise enter the filtered wine and maybe impart a taste if any quantity were to be present.

The loss of wine from filtering should be negligible but, of course, if you cannot bottle it right away do not forget to top up the vessel just as you would after racking.

SUMMING UP

1. Always sulphite a batch of wine immediately fermentation ceases and rack within a few days, topping up the storage vessel. Thereafter, rack at least twice at three to four month intervals.
2. Pectin and starch hazes should not be a problem as the relevant enzymes should be added at the must preparation stage. Check hazes for protein matter, first using Bentonite, and if necessary follow this using a proprietary wine fining gel.
3. Never use metal vessels, only those advocated; brief contact with metal kitchen utensils is of course permissible during the must preparation stage.
4. During bulk storage try to keep as steady a temperature as possible, preferably about 50 to 60°F (10 to 15.5°C) and choose a darkened place, certainly away from direct sunlight.
5. Always use a dark vessel for bulk storage unless the storage area is really dark. Never store wine in direct sunlight.
6. Thoroughly cork vessels for bulk storage. Do not use rubber bungs.
7. Certainly filter your wines but do not expect the filter to work miracles. Do as much clearing as possible before filtering and filter to obtain star brightness.
8. When filtering, do everything possible to exclude air from contact with the wine.
9. Wash the filter thoroughly immediately before use to prevent particles on the outlet side from entering the filtered wine. Sterilize the filter immediately after use.
10. Top up storage vessels after filtering, unless bottling is under-taken immediately.

CHAPTER 9

FINAL ADJUSTMENTS, BOTTLING AND BOTTLE STORAGE

Good recipes reduce the need for pre-bottling adjustments to a minimum and in the majority of instances no manipulation of the ingredients or blending will be necessary.

The main pre-bottling adjustment is the addition of sweetening sugar, or proprietary sweetening agent. In addition it may be necessary to adjust the acid and tannin contents, though these adjustments should only be marginal as a reasonably accurate assessment will already have been made when the must was prepared.

STANDARDIZING ADJUSTMENTS

SUGAR The simplest way to adjust sugar content is by direct measurement from the hydrometer, or saccharometer scales. The sweeter the wine the higher its specific gravity due to the sugar which has been added. And, knowing what its specific gravity needs to be for the degree of sweetness required, it becomes an easy matter to determine how much sugar per gallon (5 litres) needs to be added. Alternatively adjustments may be made to taste — the palate is the final adjudicator to all questions concerning the quality of a wine.

ACID In the case of both juice and pulp musts, the acid level will increase during fermentation, but it will reduce again during maturation. Due to the variables involved, if you are in any doubt about the acidity, measure again after fermentation is complete. The acid level should never be checked *immediately* following fermentation and prior to bulk storage, as at this stage, the wine is likely to contain a very considerable quantity of dissolved carbon dioxide (CO_2) which being acid in nature, will falsify the result. Ensure that the acid level is approximately correct at the preparation stage so that a bold, infection-free, fermentation is assured. Appendix I shows the recommended acidity in ppt (parts per thousand relative to sulphuric acid; although it does not occur in wine it is adopted as a standard for measuring purposes) for a range of wine styles. There is some variance between winemakers as to the correct acid level for a given style but figures considerably higher than those stated may render the wine unacceptable. However, there are some who clearly prefer a somewhat higher level as is evidenced by the growing popularity of some German wines. Certainly a reasonable acid level gives a wine a zest which stimulates the palate and frequently differentiates between the experienced and the novice vintner. Many drinkers often quite wrongly mistake the 'bite' provided by acid for a high level of alcohol. Certainly, wines which are under-acid are unacceptable and, within reason, too much is better than too little. If a wine is found to be a little too high in acid it is as well to leave things alone, especially if lengthy maturing is intended. If, however, the acid level is unacceptably high, it can be reduced. Until recently the generally accepted method has been to add precipitated chalk (calcium carbonate), but this is a somewhat messy process and it is finally necessary to remove the chalk deposit. Furthermore, its use needs to be rather limited if a chalky taste is not to be imparted to the wine. An acid reducing solution has become available recently which is easier and cleaner to use and is much more effective. Both products are available from all good homebrew outlets. Another way to reduce excessive acidity is to blend the wine with one known to be too low in this respect.

Appendix II shows the relationship of the three fruit acids against sulphuric acid. Hence, if it were calculated that 1 g of sulphuric acid would make up the necessary strength, then 1.43 g of citric acid per gallon (5 litres) would be required, and so on. Indeed, it may be decided to add a combination of acids in proportion, but in making up acid levels citric acid is very commonly used, especially if tartaric and/or malic acid are already present, as this is always well appreciated by the palate. Appendix III is a table which can be used satisfactorily to determine the acid requirement, either at the must preparation or final adjustment stages. As an example, assume that you have made a sweet red or white wine and a titration test indicates that the acid level is 3.0 ppt. It will be seen from Appendix I that the acid level for this particular style is recommended as being 5 ppt. Therefore there is a deficiency of 2.0 ppt. In column one against 2.0 ppt, it is shown in columns two, three and four that

13 g, 14 g and $12\frac{1}{2}$ g of citric, tartaric or malic acid respectively will be required per gallon to make up the deficiency. Or a proportion of each of these. Assuming you have made a 5-gallon (23-litre) batch and you decide to make up the deficiency with tartaric acid, then the amount to add is $14 \times 5 = 70$ g. A figure a little higher than this may be used if lengthy maturing is envisaged.

TANNIN Tannin imparts an element of astringency to a wine. It is recognizable by a distinctive sense of dryness on the palate, teeth and gums. Tannin abounds in red wines and is an essential part of it. It is not practicable for the amateur to measure tannin content but the exact amount present is not crucially important. When the wine is made, fined, filtered and adjusted, tasting should give a good indication as to whether or not it is lacking in this respect. Certainly, if the tannin level is very high, its excess presence will be unmistakable. If there is a deficiency the wine will tend to be insipid and lacking in astringency.

Tannin may be reduced by the addition of wine fining gel, which causes it to precipitate, but some experimentation will be required here in order to assess the necessary quantity. This is indeed another use of finings quite apart from their more recognized purpose of clearing hazes, but it should not be used on a routine basis for reducing the tannin level.

BLENDING

Very occasionally, no matter how carefully we try to balance and prepare our musts or how well we manage the fermentation and subsequent operations, a poor wine will result. We may then resort to blending. One of the fascinations of winemaking is the remarkable complexity of changes which ensue during and after fermentation and of which we know very little. It is not surprising, then, that occasionally we may produce something which does not come up to expectation. Clearly, when a wine is unacceptable it is because it may be deficient or excessive in some respects, and blending with a product which has opposing faults must surely bring about some improvement. For instance, one which is insipid may be extremely low in tannin and blending with an elderberry wine which has spent too long on the pulp may well bring about very considerable improvement. Blending is usually more complicated than mixing equal volumes of deficient and excessive wines — as it is unlikely that one brew would be excessive in a factor by the same amount that another is lacking in that characteristic. Blending can involve one to one, one to two, or even one to three or more. It is advisable to carry out small scale experiments to determine the volumes necessary to achieve the correct balance, before committing the bulk of your wines.

Furthermore, there are considerations of colour. A good red can have a considerable amount of white wine added to it and still be regarded as a red. Even more can be added and it will still produce a very acceptable rosé; but the smallest addition of red to a white will completely ruin its colour. Golden wines, such as some made from oranges, look worse than whites when a red is added.

Once a few wines are available for blending the scope is quite enormous, and many pleasant sessions can be spent in such a way. Even good wines, which may not obviously require blending, can be married with other good wines to create something really superb.

Lastly, it must be remembered that wines that are blended because they are deficient or excessive in some way may have ceased fermentation rather early, and could re-commence fermentation when that deficiency has been made good by blending. Newly blended wines should be kept for a while in a vessel fitted with an airlock, otherwise a fractured bulk vessel may well result. The winemaker should not try to prevent further fermentation, and sulphiting should only be resorted to when all visible activity has ceased. After blending a new sediment may form and new hazes may also appear, so that racking, haze treatment and filtering may again be required.

Following blending, a good period of bulk storage will again be required so that the wines can marry completely and any obvious activity can run its course.

In blending wines of differing alcoholic strength you will no doubt wish to assess the final figure. So far we have considered alcoholic strength on a percentage volume/volume basis of the whole, and in knowing the strength of each of the wines used the final figure can be simply calculated using the following expression:

$$\text{Final volume of alcohol/volume of wine} = \frac{(A \times X) + (B \times Y)}{A + B}$$

Where: A = Number of measured volumes of wine A
B = Number of measured volumes of wine B
X = V/V strength of wine A
Y = V/V strength of wine B

Similarly, if three wines are blended together the expression is simply extended thus:

$$\text{Final Volume/Volume} = \frac{(A \times X) + (B \times Y) + (C \times Z)}{A + B + C}$$

Where: C = Number of measured volumes of wine C
Z = V/V strength of wine C

The expression can be similarly extended to include any number of wines in one blending.

Example:
Six volumes of wine A (13%) are blended with two volumes of wine B (15%) and four volumes of wine C (12%). The above expression then becomes:

$$\text{Final Volume/Volume} = \frac{(6 \times 13) + (2 \times 15) + (4 \times 12)}{6 + 2 + 4}$$

$$= \frac{78 + 30 + 48}{12}$$

$$= \frac{156}{12} = 13\%$$

FORTIFYING

A fortified wine is one which has an alcoholic strength in excess of that which can be obtained by normal fermentation methods. Port and Sherry come into this category. It has already been explained that the alcohol tolerance of yeast does not normally exceed 16 or 17%. If we wish to increase the alcoholic strength of our wines beyond this value it will be necessary to resort to fortifying. This is normally undertaken by the addition of a neutral flavoured spirit such as vodka or a spirit such as brandy which contributes to the final character of the wine. It is clear that quite a considerable amount of spirit is required to increase alcohol strength for fortifying purposes and, as commercially produced spirit is extremely expensive, acquiring the alcohol level in this way tends to defeat what is one of the home winemaker's main objectives. Clearly, any wine intended for fortification will be pushed as far as possible by natural fermentation and, even then, only the best wines should be considered for fortifying.

To calculate the amount of proof spirit which needs to be added to a wine a method known as the Pearson Square (and occasionally referred to as St. Andrew's Cross) is often used. However, I much prefer use of the simple formula given below:

$$U = \frac{V (a - b)}{(c - a)}$$

Where U = Volume of spirit required
V = Volume of the wine to be fortified
a = Intended alcoholic strength (V/V)
b = Initial alcoholic strength (V/V)
c = Alcoholic strength of the spirit (V/V)

Let us now consider an example:
Assume that we have 1 gallon (5 litres) of wine having an alcoholic strength of 15% V/V, and we wish to fortify it to a level of 20% using a 40% V/V spirit.
Substituting in the formula:

$$U = \frac{8 (20 - 15)}{40 - 20} = \frac{8 \times 5}{20} = 2$$

Hence, 1 gallon (5 litres) of the wine will require 2 pints (1.14 litres) of spirit to raise the alcohol to the desired level.

BOTTLING AND BOTTLE DRESSING

During the period of final adjustment you will no doubt have enjoyed the experience of a tasting session, and now it is time to bottle the wine. Bottling allows for a further period of maturing and the wine can be divided into convenient quantities for subsequent serving. Bottles should be obtained long before they are required.

There are many commercial varieties, some of which are not suitable for amateur winemakers. The varieties having screw caps or flanged corks should be rejected. So should the heavy pressure type used for Champagne. In fact, for simplicity use only the types shown on page 29: from left to right they are Bordeaux clear, Bordeaux dark, burgundy and hock.

Bordeaux: This is a bottle of 700 ml (70 cl) capacity. Six are required to bottle 1 gallon (5 litres). It has distinctive square shoulders and is generally green-tinted for red wine and clear for white wine. It is normal for them to have a 'punted' base; (the degree dependent upon where it was produced) but this feature is of no real significance. The punt is not nearly so marked as in the case of Champagne bottles, where this feature is necessary to provide pressure vessel characteristics.

Burgundy: This bottle is of similar capacity to that above but has long shoulders and is almost invariably green-tinted. Very occasionally, white bottles are available in this style but these are something of an oddity. It also has a punted base.

Hock: A tall elegant-looking bottle, with sides tapering gently up to the neck. It stems essentially from Germany and is popular in brown, green and white, the latter enhancing the appearance of white and rosé wines. It has a capacity similar to those above but is taller, and smaller in diameter.

The type one chooses will be largely dependent upon the pattern of production, what is available and what facilities one has for storage. I now reject the hock bottle because this happens to be a wine style I rarely buy, so that the few bottles I might acquire would appear as something of an oddity in the storage racks. It is a sensible idea to concentrate initially on acquiring green bottles, for whilst it is quite satisfactory and acceptable to put white wines in green bottles, reds should never be stored in clear ones. And if one is really desperate and needs to purchase empty bottles from homebrew shops or chain stores, then it is the Bordeaux style which seems to be universally available in both green and clear glass. This is an expensive way of acquiring empty bottles, though, and if you frequent a local restaurant, or better still a steakhouse, you may well be able to obtain all the bottles you need by having a quiet word with the Manager. Do not expect him to accommodate you there and then; he may well invite you back on a Saturday or Sunday morning following a previous busy evening, when he will be only too glad for you to relieve him of a proportion of his refuse! Often 50 or 60 bottles of the right sort can be acquired in this way.

All bottles, whether newly acquired or otherwise, should always be thoroughly washed and labels removed after use, before putting aside for subsequent re-filling. Bottles left unwashed soon acquire patches of mould which are quite difficult to remove and this, together with removal of labels and seals, makes for a very tedious job when some 30 bottles or more need to be dealt with immediately prior to a bottling session. Even so, bottle cleanliness is well served by an occasional soak in sterilant such as Chempro SDP. However, bottles must be very thoroughly rinsed following this treatment as none of this solution must find its way into the finished wine.

When bottling, the number of bottles required should be counted out, washed using plenty of warm water and washing-up liquid and thoroughly rinsed free of all soap traces. A bottle brush should be used in this operation — see illustration on page 31. Following this, one of the bottles should then be quarter filled with 1% campden solution — see Chapter Four — and, having thoroughly shaken this around to sterilize it, the solution should then be transferred to the second bottle and so on until all have been similarly treated. Each bottle should be put aside, preferably upside down, or alternatively a small piece of cling film may be drawn across its opening until you are ready to fill it.

During the washing session it will also be necessary to soften and sterilize the required number of corks for an hour or so, again using a 1% campden solution. This can sometimes be a little tricky as corks are extremely buoyant in water, so they need to be weighted down in some way. However, they are often supplied in a plastic bag and a method I use, provided the bag is sound, is to open a corner carefully and pour campden solution into it. The corner of the bag is then twisted up, having first removed any air space, and held in this position by means of a wire tie. The bag may then be placed in a cup or measuring jug with the opening uppermost in case of leakage. Finally, the campden solution can be poured away leaving the corks moist in the bag until each is required.

Bottling is done in much the same way as racking, excepting that the wine is syphoned from the bulk vessel directly into the bottles — which should first be arranged neatly at the lower level to facilitate filling. Some operators fit a small plastic tap to the delivery end of the plastic tube so as to gauge accurately the amount of wine directed into each bottle, but I find this tends to slow the rate of flow. I prefer to squeeze the end of the tube with the thumb and forefinger to halt the rate of flow momentarily whilst passing from one bottle to the next, and though this method exercises rather less control it is quicker. As explained earlier, the less contact with oxygen the better and so it is preferable to fill the bottles as quickly as possible to minimize any tendency to bottle sickness. Though the bottles may not be accurately filled by this method the final adjustment can be made very simply by topping up with a little of the wine taken into a jug. Each bottle should be filled to a level which will leave an air space of approximately $\frac{5}{8}-\frac{3}{4}$ inch (16—19mm) below the cork when it is finally driven home.

When the wine is safely in the bottle the wetted corks must be fitted without delay. To do this it is best to use one of the many cheap corking tools now available. For most home winemakers the type illustrated on page 31 will serve admirably well. Anything more elaborate is an unnecessary extravagance unless really large quantities are to be handled. In the type advocated, a softened cork is placed into the barrel and the plunger fitted; the tool is then placed on top of the bottle and a downwards pressure exerted. This squeezes the cork to a somewhat smaller diameter and thus eases it into the neck of the bottle.

However, a word of warning here. It will be seen that, though these tools are all similar in design, quite a few have a pressure pad shaped for convenient use with the heel of the hand, and the intention is that the bottle be placed at a low level, say on the floor, where the operator can position himself above, thus being able to exert considerable downwards pressure. This can be dangerous. Operating in this fashion, a bottle can very easily topple over or skid on the floor, and I know a man who sustained very serious cuts requiring hospital treatment caused by such an incident, when his hand went down into broken glass backed by his full weight. It is far better, and safer, to place the bottle on a kitchen table and gently drive the plunger home, using a mallet or a hammer.

To do this, place the bottle immediately over a table leg so that the table top cannot 'spring' when the blows are delivered. If a mallet is not available and a hammer has to be used, use a large one. It is better to deliver light blows with a larger hammer than to make wild swipes with a small one. Even a watchmaker uses a large hammer! If a corking tool is not available, use a mallet, or flogger, to drive the corks home directly, but this is less satisfactory and, of course, in this case a hammer must not be used otherwise the neck of the bottle will become damaged.

It merely remains to wipe the bottles clean and dry, and to add some bottle dressing. The first is some form of cap over the cork. This will enhance the finished appearance and prevent the cork from drying out. Typical examples are shown in the illustration on page 31. Some are of a plastic push-over type, some are aluminium foil and yet others require to be heat-shrunk into position. The latter give a very professional appearance but are more expensive. All are available in a variety of colours, and even if you have not been successful in matching up all your bottles, at least ensure that you fit matching bottle caps for any particular brew so that it can be readily identified in storage.

Lastly comes labelling, and this is very important. There must be sufficient information given on any label to make the bottle contents identifiable in every detail; bottles should never be put into storage with only your memory to rely on as to contents. Remember, wines may be in storage for a very considerable period of time!

A variety of labels is available to the home winemaker, but do not try to fool yourself or others by using an obviously incorrect label. I prefer a decorative label which enhances the finished appearance tastefully, but which gives an absolutely free hand so far as description is concerned. In addition to description, the date that the wine was first committed to bulk storage should be added and I find that the finished specific gravity is the best reminder to indicate the level of sweetness. This can be added quite unobtrusively in a corner somewhere. Acid content in parts per thousand (ppt) and alcohol content may also be added as a future guide.

Certainly use a label of some sort, so that accurate information may be recorded. Rolls of perforated, tear-off sticky labels can be purchased very cheaply in a variety of sizes from most good stationers.

BOTTLE STORAGE

The bottles should be stored horizontally or as near as is practical. There is such a variety of storage racking available to the amateur these days that it would be quite pointless to try to discuss all their relative merits. Some take the form of collapsible wooden frames which look like trellis work, others are available in a combination of wooden blocks and slats, and there are quite a number of types formed solely from nylon or PVC-coated wire. They are available in many combinations of size and some are designed for extension as and when required. This latter feature is very useful.

Regardless of the exact angle of tilt each rack provides, they all enable the bottles to be stored so that the wine is actually wetting the cork. This is important, for if bottles are stored upright the corks dry out, causing them to shrink and allow air to enter and oxidise the wine. However, it is as well to take some note of the actual angle of repose. Some angle the bottles with necks slightly upwards, others horizontal, and yet others angle the necks in a downwards direction. Though the latter can be regularly seen in drinking establishments, I believe those angling the bottle slightly upwards are to be preferred. In this way any sediment which may form in the bottle (and this is a distinct possibility, especially if one's storage conditions are not ideal) will drop to the lowest point, which is the bottom of the bottle. Tilted the other way, the sediment will settle in the bottle neck or shoulder, and will be diffused back into the bulk when the bottle is opened.

Effective storage racks may be made at home by adapting old bookcases or even purchasing some of the relatively inexpensive packaged furniture. They should have a back fitted, preferably of hardboard, in order to provide the necessary rigidity, as a large quantity of bottles are very heavy. In addition, each shelf should be strengthened by regular fixings to the back panel. It is also possible

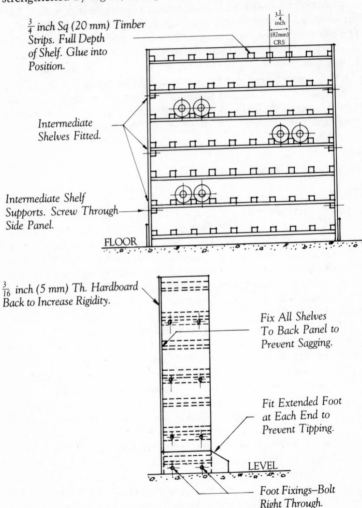

Suggested Conversion of Bookshelf Unit for Wine Bottle Storage.

to fit intermediate shelves, thus increasing the storage capacity. In this way a bookshelf of even modest dimension can be adapted to accommodate a surprising number of bottles.

The figure opposite shows how a 3 × 3ft (90 × 90 cm) bookshelf can be adapted to store wine bottles by fitting intermediate shelves and a number of rectangular wooden bars as supports. The bars can be positioned firmly at measured distances on the shelves using a little two-part cement in a couple of places on each. It will be seen that a bookshelf of this modest size will accommodate some 63 bottles, which is almost 9 gallons (40 litres) of wine. Note the size of the timber bars $\frac{3}{4}$ inch (20 mm) square and the distance of $3\frac{1}{4}$ inches (82 mm) between centres are both important dimensions. Deviation from these may mean that the bottles will not lie correctly.

SUMMING UP

1. Always carry out standardizing adjustments immediately before bottling, and do not forget to sulphite, particularly before filtering, in order to minimize the possibility of over oxidation.
2. Try to use a suitable balance for small acid measurements but if not available at least use proprietary measuring spoons.
3. If using precipitated chalk, use sparingly.
4. By all means try your hand at blending; you may be very pleasantly surprised. But do not bottle immediately following.
5. Due to the expense, only fortify wines in very special cases. To minimize the amount of spirit to be added, produce as much alcohol by natural fermentation as possible.
6. Always try to match up your bottles for any one brew or at least ensure matching bottle caps and labels, clearly marking the latter so that the batch is readily recognizable in storage.
7. Always rinse bottles immediately after use, wash thoroughly and sulphite before re-filling.
8. Do not store red wines in clear glass bottles.
9. Always use straight sided corks of good quality, softening and fitting them in the manner prescribed.
10. Always store corked bottles in a near horizontal position and try to maintain steady storage conditions.

CHAPTER 10

SERVING

In working to the recommendations in the preceding chapters, much care will have been taken to produce a quality product and now, at this stage, the most important of all, it would be folly not to continue to lavish care and attention upon the wine. This is the moment of truth, and yet even here much can be done to create the right impression. There are many people with very fixed ideas about what is traditional in the serving of wine and when a particular style should or should not be consumed. Obviously, if one is presenting a meal based on a delicately flavoured meat or fish it would be quite foolish to overpower it with a rich, robust sweet red, and conversely there is nothing worse than to take a mouthful of a really dry red in the midst of a painstakingly prepared sweet.

There are those who are not familiar with drinking wine and, having a sweet tooth, conclude that a really dry example is quite unpalatable, not realizing that the deliberate intention here is to stimulate the palate so as to better appreciate the dish being offered. A little gentle but unembarrassing advice may be given here. However, having said that, there should be no rule whatsoever today about what should or should not be consumed on any occasion. In the end it must be a matter of personal choice.

DECORKING AND DECANTING

Red wines often throw a sediment, due to oxidation of tannins, and this must be removed before serving: an operation called decanting. Any sediment which may have formed during storage will already have dropped to the bottom of the bottle. If the sediment becomes disturbed, stand the bottle upright for at least 24 hours before serving. Where this is not possible the next best course is to stand the bottle in a serving cradle for a couple of hours. It should hold a single bottle at much the same angle as that advocated for storage and is convenient for subsequent pouring.

Next, remove the capsule, making sure that the bottle is not twisted around or shaken in any way. To do this, a sharp pointed knife should be used. Remove the cork.

To decant the wine, take a clean, empty bottle or a decanter and pour the wine steadily into it. With care, all the sediment will be left in the shoulder of the bottle and very little of the wine will have been wasted. Of course, if there is no sediment this operation will not be necessary, but wine should always be poured carefully. It should never be poured like milk from a milk bottle into a jug!

CORKSCREWS

Fitting corks was discussed in the previous chapter and from what was said it will be clear that some effort is required in order to fit them. It follows then that a degree of effort is also required to remove them, and whilst this is well within the capability of all but the frailest, it must be done carefully, without disturbing the sediment. There are many designs of corkscrew on the market which recognize this fact, but there are one or two other factors which also need to be considered. The illustration on page 108 shows a number of corkscrews; it certainly does not cover the whole range, but they serve to illustrate the points discussed.

A factor which is rarely considered when purchasing a corkscrew is the screw itself, yet this is very important. In most of the early designs it was made from heavy-gauge steel wire wound into helical form, rather like a coil spring, and having a sharpened end. All the corkscrews illustrated have a business end like this, excepting that shown on the extreme right. The steel helix is ideal, for in this form the screw 'worms' its way into the cork without creating any associated damage. Thus the cork becomes very positively held and, even if the screw finally protrudes on the far side, no cork particles are likely to drop into the wine. However, today many quite elaborate corkscrews have appeared on the market; some are formed in a cheap, zinc-based material which, whilst lending itself admirably to low cost manufacture, has very little strength. Accordingly a helically formed screw of this material would be quite useless and so a number of alternative forms have appeared. That on the right in page 108 is an example.

Five Popular Corkscrews in Everyday Use

In fairness, this particular screw form appears to function quite satisfactorily, but any corkscrew offered which has a screw remotely resembling a carpenter's gimlet should be rejected as it may well serve better to drill a hole in the cork rather than to get hold of it cleanly! I once heard a complaint in a restaurant about cork particles in a wine, and the wine waitress explained that it had happened quite a lot lately and that it was due to a consignment of wine having a bad batch of corks! When she returned with a second bottle it was patently obvious to me that her corkscrew was the culprit! It was just like one I had been using.

On the left hand side of the illustration is the original, general-purpose corkscrew which, whilst having a good screw form, is nevertheless generally unsatisfactory due to the manhandling required in its use. The second illustration is of a folding, portable type which is perhaps useful to keep with a picnic set. But, when the screw cover is removed and threaded through the body of the screw to be used as a handle, it has the same faults as the previous example. Number three is also of the folding variety but is a better design, some mechanical advantage being afforded, as the handle is used as a lever and less effort is required to remove the cork and so there is less likelihood of disturbing any sediment there may be in the bottle. Again, this is a good example to carry in a car or picnic set as it is a useful combination tool being also designed as a bottle cap remover. The fourth example is, in my view, by far the best of those illustrated. It is robustly constructed, of suitable materials, and designed correctly in every detail. When it is firmly screwed into the cork the latter can be removed quite effortlessly by simply turning the lower screw. The last example, which has already received some consideration, is very ingeniously designed. There are many other examples, and at least one which injects a gas pressure onto the inside of the bottle which, when sufficiently high, will virtually blow out the cork. However, I have heard of this type breaking the bottle, which is expensive, clearly disconcerting and potentially dangerous. Its use cannot be recommended.

PRESENTATION

Throughout this book both clarity and bouquet have been stressed as important adjuncts to the taste of any wine style. And so presentation is naturally very important as people will see the wine before they taste it. It is true to say that a favourable review of clarity and bouquet alone undoubtedly go a considerable way towards the ultimate appreciation. Presentation must in no way detract and though a little skilful dressing up may be permissible, or on occasions even desirable, an 'overkill' situation must be avoided. The choice of glass, and even the salver upon which it is presented, should therefore receive consideration.

Wine served on a silver or silver-plated salver is invariably well received, as the brilliant yet soft reflections that only silver can bestow are almost universally appreciated. But the effect can be completely ruined by over-ostentation; a minimum of ornamentation gives the brightest and clearest images and is therefore most unlikely to arrest one's interest from the colour and clarity of the wine itself.

The choice of glass is important. Clarity can best be appreciated when viewed through an absolutely clear glass and so coloured glasses should always be avoided. However, there are few examples having coloured stems and, provided that the colour is complementary to the wine, these are acceptable, but certainly any colouring of the bowl or balloon itself should be beyond consideration. Admittedly though, on occasions some may wish to serve wine in a lead crystal cut glass rather than a clear one; this can be very satisfying. Fortunately, today's designs are generally less elaborate than they were half a century or more ago and the simpler, bolder and more crisply cut patterns of modern glass seem to create an added sparkle rather than to detract. Etched glasses rather than the deep-cut variety can also be very attractive without detracting from the clarity of the wine. Conversely, some of the lower cost ornamental lead crystal is not really cut at all in the true sense. By comparison, the facets are not nearly so crisply defined and the design is frequently overdone. These do nothing whatsoever to enhance presentation.

Small glasses should be used for fortified or aperitif wines, but in all other cases glasses should be large enough to hold a generous helping without overfilling. About two-thirds full is invariably correct. The glass should tend to curve inwards towards the top, so as to contain and concentrate the bouquet. Red wines should be served in short-stemmed glasses, so that the more volatile elements which promote bouquet are liberated and driven off by warmth from the hand. A similarly styled glass but larger, for even more generous helpings, is called a goblet.

White and rosé styles should be served chilled and ideally should be presented in a long-stemmed glass. In this case only the stem should be handled so that warmth from the hand is not transferred to the chilled wine. Often too, condensation forms on the bowl of the glass containing chilled wine and for appearance sake this is better left undisturbed.

SUMMING UP

1. There should be no fixed rules about wine styles to be served with certain dishes, but try initially to observe some convention. For very sound reasons wine guides are drawn up on a basis of what is considered to be generally best for certain categories of food.
2. Aim at dry white wines for poultry and fish, with perhaps a higher acid level in the case of fish prepared in oil or fat.
3. For stronger flavoured, red meats aim at dry red wines which contain higher levels of tannin. A slightly sweeter wine may be consumed with pork which is often served with a sweet apple sauce.
4. Handle the bottle to be opened with extreme care, so as not to disturb any sediment, and decant carefully.
5. Always use a good quality corkscrew, preferably with a clean simple helix and one which will remove corks with a minimum of physical effort.
6. For presentation, use a small, simple silver or silver-plated salver if possible.
7. Always serve wines in clear glass and maybe occasionaly in clear cut lead crystal glass. Avoid the use of coloured or tinted glass.
8. Use the correct glass for the particular wine style being served.
9. Charge glasses to two-thirds full only.

CHAPTER 11

THE HYDROMETER OR SACCHAROMETER

The hydrometer is a simple instrument used to measure the specific gravity or density of a liquid, a sample of which is first charged into a trial jar. That is to say, it compares the weight of a given volume of a liquid with that of the same volume of water. The specific gravity of water is 1.000. Or, that is, one cubic centimetre of water weighs one gram. Weights and measures were standardized so that the weight of one cubic centimetre of water was called one gram, hence the weight of any liquid can be compared with that of the commonest and most important liquid available to man. If a liquid is known to have a specific gravity of 1.25 then one cubic centimetre of that liquid will weigh 1.25 g. In fact, any given volume of the liquid will be 25% heavier than that of the same volume of water. This leads to the second way of expressing any given value. If the specific gravity is said to be 1.25 then the gravity (omitting the word specific) is said to be 25 or 25% heavier than water.

Page 112 shows an hydrometer used in conjunction with a trial jar. It can be seen that the hydrometer consists merely of a glass stem which is graduated in figures representing specific gravity, and at one end of which is an enlarged weighted glass bulb so that it floats vertically. Because it floats at a higher or lower level, according to the specific gravity of the liquid to which it is applied, the specific gravity of that liquid can be read directly from the graduations on its stem.

Dissolving sugar in water or a must increases the specific gravity of the liquid. As fermentation of a must proceeds, gradually transforming the sugar to alcohol, so the specific gravity, which will start off at a figure higher than 1.000 beause of the dissolved sugar content, must fall. Because the specific gravity of water is 1.000 and that of ethyl alcohol is less than 1.000, it follows that the overall

111

specific gravity of the resulting wine is likely to be less than 1.000 should all, or most of, the sugar be transformed into alcohol. Many of the very dry table wines we make will finish with a specific gravity of 0.990.

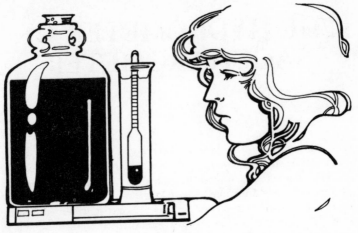

Reading Specific Gravity from the Hydrometer/Saccharometer
Eyes in line with surface level of liquid

But there are other factors which may have a marginal effect on the readings; these are mainly caused by the ingredients in the fruit and the quantity used. Do these have a specific gravity of more or less than 1.000? Generally speaking, they may be regarded as being in the order of 1.000 and therefore they are not likely to significantly affect our readings and so for all practical purposes they may be ignored. It follows, however, that for a number of reasons the readings we take with our hydrometer are not going to be absolutely accurate.

Hydrometers are made for all manner of purposes. Many are very cheap, having only a limited degree of accuracy whilst others are manufactured to provide very accurate readings such that their scales are so enlarged as to involve more than one instrument in order to cover the range. However, there is no need whatsoever for such accuracy and its related additional expense for the purpose of home winemaking. Accordingly, a number of manufacturers now market at low cost what is termed a saccharometer (or sugar measurer) which is identical with the hydrometer described but includes extra graduated scales adjacent to the specific gravity scale to measure both sugar content and corresponding alcohol potential, without our having to calculate them from the specific gravity reading. These are an absolute boon to the home winemaker and to my mind they provide all the information he is ever likely to need. I consider such an instrument to be wholly adequate and quite indispensable.

However, if you have available an hydrometer rather than a saccharometer it can still be used satisfactorily in conjunction with the table shown in Appendix V. This shows the sugar content and alcohol potential against any specific gravity reading, corresponding to the scales directly marked on saccharometer barrels. It may vary very slightly from similar charts quoted by others authorities, but it is well within the limits of the experimental error of the hydrometer.

Temperature

Another factor which can affect accuracy is temperature. Heating liquids renders them less dense, as they expand slightly. So the hydrometer or saccharometer will tend to float at a lower level than normal in a hot liquid. However, the differences are so marginal that providing the readings are taken between 55 to 65°F (13 to 18°C) they can be ignored. The hydrometers and saccharometers advocated here are not suitable for use at elevated temperatures anyway.

The hydrometer is read as shown on page 112. Due to the shape and size of the bulb the glass is very thin at the lower tip, so take care not to drop the instrument into the liquid, particularly when the gravity reading is very low as at the end of fermentation. The bulb may fracture on contact with the bottom of the trial jar should it strike it with any degree of force. Always ensure that there is sufficient liquid in the trial jar to enable the instrument to float freely. Remember fermenting or recently-fermented musts will contain a considerable quantity of carbon dioxide, so that the hydrometer will float at an incorrectly high level. The way to avoid this is to move it up and down a few times in the liquid, finally giving it a brisk spin so as to centrifuge the bubbles from around the bulb.

When observing the surface in order to take a reading, it will be seen that the liquid adjacent to the wall of the trial jar and the stem of the instrument curves slightly upwards due to surface tension. This creates a surface form referred to as a 'meniscus' and the correct reading is obtained from the point on the scale corresponding to the generally flat surface between the upturned edges. The illustration shows where to look in order to obtain a correct reading, normally with the eyes viewing directly across the liquid surface. It is difficult, if not impossible, to see a flat surface in musts containing pulp and it is likely that the pulp will not permit floating at the correct level anyway. So, if it is required to measure the gravity of such a must, it should first be filtered or strained.

It goes almost without saying that the hydrometer or saccharometer should be washed before and after use and that for storage it should be dried and kept safely in the container in which it is supplied.

SUMMING UP

1. Remember the difference in the expressions gravity and specific gravity and do not get them confused.
2. For simplicity of use, always acquire a wine saccharometer rather than an hydrometer, though these names are often interchangeable amongst winemakers.
3. Keep hydrometer or saccharometer and trial jar in container supplied.
4. Do not subject trial jar or instrument to very hot water. Preferably, rinse in campden solution.
5. Do not drop the instrument into the test sample.
6. Always agitate and spin the instrument in the must or wine before reading.
7. Take readings, as on page 112, using the 'flat' part of the meniscus as the correct level.
8. Allow for any difficulty there may be in reading pulp musts.
9. Allow for sugar in pulp which cannot be measured on the instrument.
10. Use the instrument to devise your own recipes as outlined in Chapter Fourteen.

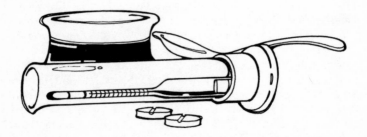

CHAPTER 12

DETERMINING ACID CONTENT BY TITRATION

Many of the simpler or beginner's recipes tend to ignore wine acids, presumably assuming that the acid level already present in the fruit will be about right; but measurement and adjustment is both simple and inexpensive and because the correct level of acids bestows extensive benefits in fermentation, ageing and final appreciation, their presence in correct proportion is certainly a most important matter. This one feature alone probably does more to account for the superb results obtained by some home winemakers, compared with the disappointing efforts produced by others.

The method of measurement is referred to as titration, but we must not allow ourselves to be put off by that! Remember, it is a term used by chemists and they are renowned for using high-sounding words, even for the humblest substances and simplest of operations. The test, which is carried out on a minute sample of the must or wine, employs the principle of using an alkali to neutralize the acid. In a laboratory a liquid is checked for free acid content by taking a measured volume of the liquid and measuring the amount of sodium hydroxide solution (caustic soda) of a known strength needed to neutralize the acid. Once the amount of caustic soda solution required to neutralize the acid is known only a simple arithmetic calculation is necessary to determine the amount of free acid present. The neutralization point is observed by first adding to the sample a few drops of indicator (phenolphthalein) which remains colourless until the neutralization point arrives, when a slight greyness in the sample appears and after which the sample turns purple/red if the alkali is exceeded.

Measuring the Acid

The normal laboratory titration procedure uses test tubes, pipettes, burettes and stands, together with sodium hydroxide of accurately known strength and thus provides results of very great accuracy. Happily, however, whilst it is highly desirable to be able to measure and adjust the acid in our wines to generally accepted levels, laboratory standards of accuracy are not necessary. It will be recalled that the acid level increases during fermentation and decreases again during ageing and storage, so there are quite a number of factors which will influence the level of acid our wines finally contain at the consumption stage. Accordingly, one of the wine acid testing kits specially prepared for the home winemaker and employing the same operating principle as that described is all that will *ever* be needed. Such a kit can be obtained from any good homebrew shop. Each contains a test tube, graduated measuring dropper, the chemicals outlined and complete instructions for easy use. The method of use may vary slightly from one kit to another, but all employ the same principle and are so simple to use it would be quite pointless and maybe even confusing to try to elaborate further here. The whole kit, including chemicals, will cost about 50% of one bottle of commercially produced supermarket table wine.

A few authors, mainly chemists, advocate use of laboratory-quality equipment and some recommend graduating to such equipment in due course on gaining experience, but really, no matter how exacting one wishes to be, such accuracy is quite meaningless.

At this point it would be as well to add a few words of caution. Our calculated titration results give us figures measured in parts per thousand (ppt) related to sulphuric acid. However, just as in the last chapter dealing with sugar and specific gravity it was explained why water was used as the standard of comparison so, in titration, sulphuric acid is chosen as the standard measurement of acidity. But the results obtained in no way imply that it should be used in our wines. Sulphuric acid must NEVER be used in winemaking. Use only edible acids obtainable from chemists and homebrew suppliers.

The sulphuric acid figure we calculate requires to be converted for the type of acid or acids we intend to use. Appendix II shows the relationship. The small quantity of must or wine used in any test must be discarded afterwards.

A minor difficulty which is sometimes experienced lies in testing a sample of red must or wine as the colour which is produced by the indicator when the neutral point is reached is very similar to that of the sample under test, particularly if it is elderberry-based. How-

116

ever, the standard test invariably calls for the sample to be diluted with three or four parts of distilled water before the neutralizer is added, and this renders the sample much paler in colour. If difficulty is experienced, the sample may be diluted very considerably until it becomes almost colourless. It will have no effect whatsoever on the finished result and the very slight greying of the sample, immediately prior to the colour change, can be observed quite clearly if care is taken.

One important point to remember when measuring the acidity of a juice at commencement of a must preparation, is to take into consideration the bulk of the juice at that stage. Assume the volume of juice, before extension to 1 gallon (5 litres) with water/sugar solution etc, is $2\frac{1}{2}$ pints (1.43 litres) and that its acidity is shown to be 12 ppt. Then the ultimate acidity when made up to 1 gallon (5 litres) would be:

$$\frac{12 \times 2\frac{1}{2}}{8} = \frac{30}{8} = 3\frac{3}{4} \text{ ppt}$$

Assuming that the wine style required has a final acidity of five ppt, it would be necessary to increase the acidity by $5 - 3\frac{3}{4} = 1\frac{1}{4}$ ppt. However, at the outset it may be preferred to keep the initial acidity a little on the low side, making the final adjustment before bottling, as there will be some increase in acidity during fermentation. But do not try to ferment without a good acid presence, as medicinal tasting wines can result.

In some text books you may see acidity referred to as a percentage but so long as this is noticed it is not likely to present any difficulty. Percentage merely means parts per hundred, whereas parts per thousand (ppt) are more normally encountered in acidity measurements. For example, three ppt is the same as 0.3 parts per hundred or 0.3%.

SUMMING UP

1. Always titrate a sample of must before fermentation and establish sufficient acid level to ensure a strong, vigorous fermentation.
2. Remember if pulp remains in the must it may give an incorrect answer.
3. Always titrate finished wines as soon as possible and standardize the acid content to ensure good ageing and final appreciation.
4. Do not titrate wines immediately following fermentation as the presence of CO_2 will give high acidity results.
5. Marginally high acidity may well be acceptable as ageing reduces acidity.
6. Keep all titration equipment clean and do not cross-contaminate chemicals.
7. Dispense with must and wine samples after testing. Do not re-introduce into the bulk.
8. Keep all bottle caps tightly secured and out of the way of the young and elderly.
9. Sodium hydroxide (caustic soda) is a paint remover and if spilled on work surfaces etc. must be cleared up without delay.
10. Phenolphthalein (indicator) is a weak acid but a very strong laxative, so wash hands well after use and keep well away from foodstuffs.

CHAPTER 13

TWENTY RECIPES FOR SUCCESS

All the following recipes may be undertaken without difficulty and with the utmost confidence of success using any combination of the methods previously outlined. The recipes specify the ingredients for 1-gallon (5-litre) batches, as many will opt to make this quantity or perhaps a number of differing batches of this quantity. It is a simple matter to scale-up a recipe for any desired batch size and in this regard one may well give thought to the particular wine style. For instance, many like substantial stocks of perhaps only two or three table wines whilst greater variety and therefore smaller batches are preferred in the social and dessert categories, particularly as these latter styles often require a greater quantity of the more expensive fruits. Because of abundant and inexpensive availability of the appropriate fruits, I like to carry a good stock of dry white and red table wines based on apples and elderberries respectively. And of these it is very easy to modify the white table style, making it somewhat sweeter and perhaps introducing a little red grape concentrate to make a rosé which is quite delightful with roast pork and apple sauce.

In all cases each finished gallon (5 litres) should be made up initially to no more than 7 pints (4 litres) and leaving out 1 lb (450 g) sugar so that the final amount will be ultimately adjusted with the gradual addition of (1) pint (570 ml) strong sugar solution (SSS) i.e. 1 lb (450 g) sugar dissolved in $\frac{1}{2}$ pint (285 ml) of water to form 1 pint (570 ml) concentrated solution.

In the case of pulp fermentation, it may be necessary to leave out a little more liquid, in order to leave room for the fruit cap, until the pulp is removed by straining. Always take care to see that all ingredients are accounted for in the bulk, as a common fault, especially with beginners, is to end up with too much liquid. And remember, too, that the starter represents about 1 pint (570 ml) which can make a very considerable difference, particularly when making smaller batches.

With regard to the social/dessert styles, where fermentation is being undertaken to the limit of yeast alcohol tolerance, it is important to ensure that towards the end of fermentation the water additions have been maximized so as to finish at one gallon when all SSS has been added. Fermentation will cease at around 16% V/V alcohol, so that if a dessert fermentation is proceeding with insufficient water all activity will cease at this point leaving residual sugar, and any final topping up with water would then merely dilute the alcohol content.

It should be noted that in all cases where water is warmed to dissolve sugar, the temperature should not be taken any higher than necessary and the resulting sugar solution must be allowed to cool before adding to the must. Similarly, when using warmed water to dilute the must and raise its temperature to commence fermentation, it should not be taken above 75°F (24°C) or the pectolytic enzyme will be destroyed.

APPLE

The varieties of apple suitable for winemaking are far too numerous to mention, and one can only employ what has come to be regarded as good practice — avoid using the tasteless imported variety which seem to abound in our shops these days, and use a mix of two or more of good eating and cooking varieties, even adding a few crab apples if available.

Comments regarding preparation of apples for fermentation are to be found in Chapter Six under the heading 'Hard Fruits', so no further comments are necessary here.

(1) Apple: Style, White Table Dry (Approx 12% Alc)*

> 5 lb (2.25 kg) mixed apples (e.g. 3 lb (1.5 kg) Bramleys
> and 2 lb (900 g) Coxs)
> 8 oz (225 g) grape concentrate
> $1\frac{1}{2}$ lb (680 g) sugar
> Pectolytic enzyme
> Amylase
> Yeast nutrient
> 1 × 3 mg vitamin B_1 tablet
> Liquid tannin (as supplier's instructions)
> $\frac{1}{4}$ oz (7 g) citric acid
> General purpose, Burgundy or Bordeaux yeast starter
> 1 campden tablet (or 1 tsp (5 ml) 10% stock solution)

Method

Prepare yeast starter as outlined in Chapter Seven. Wash the apples and extract the juice by crushing or pulping (first freezing apples and thoroughly thawing if this will assist) according to the equipment available. Add *immediately* to a clean and sterilized bucket containing 1 pint (570 ml) cold water into which the campden tablet has been dissolved or 10% stock solution added. Stir in the pectolytic enzyme and amylase according to supplier's instructions. Fit the lid and place aside for 24 hours. Then, very carefully, decant juice from the settled pulp, finally pressing or squeezing the pulp in a filter bag to express as much juice as possible, and transfer to fermenter. Add the grape concentrate and 6 drops grape tannin according to supplier's instructions. Dissolve 8 oz (225 g) sugar, the nutrient tablet and citric acid in a little water. Add this to the bulk and make up the whole to 6 pints (3.4 litres) with warmed water, bringing to the fermentation temperature of approximately 70 to 75°F (21 to 24°C). During this procedure do not allow the temperature to rise above 75°F (24°C). When the temperature is correct, add yeast starter and commence fermentation as already outlined. Make up the remaining 1lb (450 g) sugar as SSS and add to bulk later, finally making up to 1 gallon (5 litres) when initial fermentation subsides. Following fermentation, add one Campden tablet (or equivalent 10% Sulphite solution) and rack after two or three days. Rack and fine as necessary. Adjust acid if required, sweeten to approx 1.000 and store to mature.

This wine should have an acidity of about 4 ppt. Make a little higher if a fair period of maturing is envisaged. A sweeter rosé can be made by increasing acidity to 5 ppt, sweetening to 1.005 and using a red grape concentrate in place of the white.

(2) Apple: Style, White Dessert (Approx 16% Alc)

> 8 lb (3.64 kg) mixed windfall apples
> 1 lb (450 g) sultanas (or ½ pint 285 ml white grape concentrate)
> 1¾ lb (800 g) sugar
> Pectolytic enzyme
> Amylase
> Tronozymol nutrient (as supplier's instructions)
> Sherry or Sauternes yeast starter
> 1 campden tablet (or 1 tsp (5 ml) of 10% stock solution)

Method

Prepare yeast starter as outlined in Chapter seven. Wash apples and remove any bruised or unsound portions. Chop up or pulp, including core and peel, according to equipment available and add *immediately* to a sterilized bucket with 1 pint (570 ml) cold water into which the campden tablet has been dissolved or 10% stock solution added. Wash and mince the sultanas thoroughly and add to the bucket. Make sure that all is covered, adding a little more water if necessary, and stir in the pectolytic enzyme and amylase. Fit bucket lid and place aside for 24 hours. When starter is thoroughly active dissolve 12 oz (340 g) sugar in water and add to must. Mix in the Tronozymol nutrient, together with extra water, adjusting temperature as required to make 7 pints (4 litres) of must, including the starter, to finish at approx 75°F (24°C). Make up the remaining 1 lb (450 g) into 1 pint (570 ml) SSS and put aside for future addition. Ferment on pulp for two to three days. Strain off pulp into a filter bag and express juice thoroughly back into must. Add SSS as required to complete fermentation. Add campden tablet (or equivalent stock solution) and rack after a few days. Rack and fine as necessary. Sweeten to 1.020, or to taste. This wine may be a little high in acid but will mellow with ageing.

Note:
An apple rosé can be obtained by using red grape concentrate in place of the sultanas or white concentrate.

APRICOT

Fresh apricots are rather expensive for winemaking and therefore not one of the better propositions. Furthermore, in my view, apricots are not a particularly good medium for table wines. However, many people appear to like a dessert apricot and so a recipe for wine of this style is included. This is based on the use of tinned apricots, which are less expensive; of course, dried apricots may also be used although they tend to produce a rather gummy must.

(3) Apricot: Style, White Dessert (Approx 16% Alc)

> 3 large tins (856 g each) apricots
> 1 lb (450 g) sultanas
> $1\frac{1}{2}$ lb (680 g) sugar
> Pectolytic enzyme
> Tronozymol nutrient
> 1 tsp (5 ml) citric acid
> Sherry or Sauternes yeast starter
> 1 campden tablet (or measured stock solution)

Method

Prepare active yeast starter. Liquidize or crush can contents and add to a sterile bucket containing 1 pint (570 ml) water to which a campden tablet or stock solution has been added. Thoroughly wash and mince the sultanas and add to the bulk. Mix in the pectolytic enzyme, fit the bucket lid and place aside for 24 hours. Dissolve the 8 oz (225 g) sugar in a little warmed water and add this to the must, together with the remaining ingredients, finally making up the volume to 7 pints (4 litres) including the starter. Make up the remaining 1 lb (450 g) sugar into 1 pint (570 ml) SSS. Ferment on pulp for three to four days and pass through a sieve, transferring to a fermenter to continue under an airlock. Make SSS additions as required to finish at 1 gallon (5 litres). Campden and rack finished fermentation, and remove any heavy pulp sediment which builds up during the next two to three weeks by further rackings. Continue to rack and fine as necessary, finally sweetening to 1.020 or to taste.

BILBERRY

Bilberries may be found in this country, but searches are often quite fruitless and at best disappointing. However, they are generally available either bottled or canned from supermarkets and freezer centres and also in dried form. I prefer them bottled or canned as I feel the quality is better. They make an excellent table wine, and a dessert wine having Port style characteristics is also possible. A recipe for both styles is included. The latter benefits from a greater maturing period. Being made entirely from preserved fruits these styles can be made all year round.

(4) Bilberry: Style, Red Table Dry (Approx 12% Alc)

> 2 × 1 lb (450 g) jars bilberries
> 15 oz (425 g) tin black cherries
> 8 oz (225 g) sultanas
> $1\frac{1}{2}$ lb (675 g) sugar
> $\frac{1}{8}$ oz (4 g) citric acid
> Pectolytic enzyme
> Yeast nutrient
> 3 mg vitamin B_1 tablet
> 1 campden tablet (or measured stock solution)
> General purpose Burgundy or Bordeaux yeast starter

Method

Prepare yeast starter. Remove stones from fruit and add the fruit to a sterile bucket containing 1 pint (570 ml) water to which a campden tablet or sulphite solution has been added. Thoroughly wash and mince the sultanas and add to the bulk. Mix in the pectolytic enzyme, fit the bucket lid and place aside for 24 hours. Dissolve 8 oz (225 g) sugar in a little warmed water and add this to the must, together with the remaining ingredients, finally making up the volume to 7 pints (4 litres) including the starter. Make up the remaining 1 lb (450 g) sugar into 1 pint (570 ml) SSS. Ferment on pulp for three to four days then pass must through a sieve, transferring to a fermenter to continue under an airlock. Make SSS additions as required (and water if necessary) to finish at 1 gallon (5 litres). Campden, rack and fine as necessary.

(5) Bilberry: Style, Port Dessert (Approx 16–18% Alc)

2 × 1 lb (450 g) jars bilberries
1 pint (570 ml) red grape concentrate
1 lb (450 g) fresh elderberries
2 lb (900 g) sugar
$\frac{1}{4}$ oz (7 g) tartaric acid
Pectolytic enzyme
Tronozymol
1 campden tablet (or measured stock solution)
Port, Tokay or similar yeast starter

Method
Prepare generally as in method above, first crushing elderberries in bucket and hold back the red grape juice, adding to the remaining ingredients 24 hours later.

Note:
This recipe is rather high in sugar and, hopefully, alcohol content. Hence, some degree of sugar feeding may be required for maximum yield (see Chapter Fourteen). Finally, sweeten to taste.

BLACKBERRY

Blackberries are a good fruit for winemaking but I always feel they require something else with them. For this, elderberries are a very convenient addition — because they are high in tannin, they provide that little extra astringency and they combine to produce a good, rich red. Furthermore, they ripen together in the hedgerows with the added attraction that they come absolutely free! Only good, dark blackberries should be picked but do not collect them too late in the year. Late blackberries look good but they are invariably quite watery and tasteless, so try them for taste first.

Elderberries come in quite a number of varieties, but generally those with red stems are the better proposition. Only include berries which are really black and produce a good red juice when crushed. Again, try them before spending time picking the wrong sort. And wait until they are really ripe; sprays containing unripe berries should not be harvested as even those which appear to be ripe will not be ready for winemaking. To collect elderberries, take a walking stick and a pair of kitchen scissors. Cut off each whole spray of berries and take care not to damage the tree when pulling the branches down.

(6) Blackberry: Style, Red Table Dry (Approx 12% Alc)

2 lb (900 g) blackberries
1 lb (450 g) elderberries
8 oz (225 g) sultanas
2 lb (900 g) sugar
$\frac{1}{4}$ oz (7 g) tartaric or citric acid
Pectolytic enzyme
Yeast nutrient
1 × 3 mg vitamin B_1 tablet
1 campden tablet (or measured stock solution)
General purpose Burgundy or Bordeaux yeast starter

Method

Prepare the yeast starter. Sort and lightly wash the blackberries in small quantities to remove any livestock. Pulp and add to a sterilized bucket containing 1 pint (570 ml) cold water to which campden tablet or stock solution has been added. Using a fork, strip the elderberries from the stems, finally weighing with the stems removed. Wash and crush the berries then add to the blackberries. Wash and mince the sultanas and add to the bulk, finally stirring in the pectolytic enzyme. Place aside for 24 hours. Dissolve 1 lb (450 g) of the sugar in a little warmed water and add this, together with all remaining ingredients and water, making the total up to 7 pints (4 litres), including the starter, gradually raising the temperature by slightly warming the water additions as necessary. Make up the remaining 1 lb (450 g) sugar as SSS. Ferment on the pulp for three days (no longer) and transfer the must to a fermenter to continue under an airlock. Make SSS additions as required (and water if necessary) to finish at 1 gallon (5 litres). Finally campden, rack and fine as necessary.

(7) Blackberry and Apple: Style, Rich Rosé Dessert (Approx 16% Alc)

3 lb (1.5 kg) blackberries
4 lb (1.8 kg) mixed apples
1 lb (450 g) sultanas
2 lb (900 g) sugar
$\frac{1}{4}$ oz (7 g) citric acid
Pectolytic enzyme
Tronozymol
1 campden tablet (or measured stock solution)
Port, Tokay or similar yeast starter

Method

Prepare yeast starter. Sort and wash the blackberries as in previous recipe. Deal with apple pulping as in apple dessert recipe and add to the blackberries, together with minced sultanas. Stir in pectolytic enzyme, fit bucket lid and place aside for 24 hours. Now add remaining ingredients and again proceed to completion as outlined in the previous recipe. Rack and fine as necessary, finally sweetening to 1.020 or to taste.

BLACKCURRANT

Blackcurrants are not only high in tannin, flavour and acid, but are also rather more uncommon and expensive than many other fruits, so they are of rather less interest to many winemakers. However, good wines can be made using only a small amount of blackcurrants in combination with other fruits. Due to their very distinctive high flavour, they lend themselves better to dessert wines, but this is by no means a rule. Bananas are included in this particular wine as they have generally opposing characteristics and they provide the body required for the dessert style.

(8) Blackcurrant: Style, Rosé Dessert (Approx 16% Alc)

1 lb (450 g) blackcurrants
1 pint (570 ml) white grape juice
1 lb (450 g) over-ripe bananas
2 lb (900 g) sugar
Pectolytic enzyme
Tronozymol
1 campden tablet (or measured stock solution)
Burgundy yeast starter

Method

Prepare yeast starter. Wash the berries and crush in a sterile bucket, then add 1 pint (570 ml) water into which a campden tablet has been dissolved. Prepare a banana 'gravy' by removing the skins, chopping the fruit and adding to 2 pints (1.14 litres) water. Simmer for about 20 minutes in a closed pan or, alternatively, cook in a pressure cooker for 5 minutes. Strain off and when cool, add the 'gravy' to the other prepared fruit. Do not be put off by the appearance and colour of this 'gravy', which may tend to solidify on cooling. Mix in well, adding the pectolytic enzyme. Fit bucket lid and place aside for 24 hours. Dissolve all sugar as SSS and add half, making up the total to 7 pints (4 litres) with warm water to finish at 75°F (24°C) including the active starter. Ferment on pulp for three days, strain and press through a filter bag and continue fermentation under an airlock, adding remaining SSS as fermentation proceeds to finish at 1 gallon (5 litres). Rack and fine as necessary, finally sweetening to 1.020 or to taste.

CHERRY

Cherries produce a most acceptable wine and yet few people seem to make it. A mixture of cooking and sweet cherries is best, but if only sweet cherries are available these will be quite satisfactory. If Morello cherries are used in the mix then the total quantity advocated may be reduced. But, though cherry wine is quite distinctive in flavour, it is not overpowering and so the exact mix and/or quantity is not critical. Again, I feel this medium lends itself better to the dessert style.

(9) Cherry: Style, Red Dessert (Approx 16% Alc)

4 lb (1.8 kg) black cherries
1 lb (450 g) sultanas
2¼ lb (1.1 kg) sugar
½ oz (14 g) citric acid
Pectolytic enzyme
Tronozymol
1 campden tablet (or measured stock solution)
Burgundy, Bordeaux or similar yeast starter

Method
Prepare yeast starter. Wash the cherries and break them into a sterile bucket containing 1 pint (570 ml) water with a campden tablet added. Keep the fruit covered by adding more water as necessary. Thoroughly wash, mince and add the sultanas. Stir in the pectolytic enzyme. Fit bucket lid and place aside for 24 hours. Add the remaining ingredients, including 1¼ lb (565 g) sugar dissolved in warm water, adjusting final quantity to 7 pints (4 litres), including the starter, with warmed water to finish at approximately 75°F (24°C). Make up the remaining 1 lb (450 g) sugar into 1 pint (570 ml) SSS. Ferment on pulp for five to six days. Strain and press through filter bag to remove pulp and stones and continue fermentation to completion under an airlock adding SSS, and water if

necessary, to finish at 1 gallon (5 litres). Rack and fine as necessary, finally sweetening to 1.020 or to taste.

DAMSON

Damsons make really first class table and dessert wines and so a recipe for each is included. In my view, no good winemaker should allow any harvest to pass without making a reasonable quantity of one or other — or both. The dessert style in particular is a wonderful stock item, gradually maturing over a longer period to take on port-type characteristics. Pulp fermentation is necessary to produce a really satisfying rich red and the necessary astringency from the skins.

(10) Damson: Style, Red Dessert (Approx 16% Alc)

6 lb (2.72 kg) fully ripened damsons
1 lb (450 g) sultanas
2 lb (900 g) sugar
Pectolytic enzyme
Tronozymol
1 campden tablet (or measured stock solution)
Port or Burgundy yeast starter

Method

Prepare yeast starter. Wash all fruit thoroughly. Inspect and crush between fingers and add to a sterile bucket containing 1 pint (570 ml) water into which a campden tablet has been added. Add water as necessary to keep fruit covered. If the stones are difficult to remove from damsons allow them to remain. Mince and add the sultanas. Mix in the pectolytic enzyme, fit bucket lid and place aside for 24 hours. Dissolve 1 lb (450 g) sugar in warmed water and add this to the must with the remaining ingredients, finally making up the volume to 7 pints (4 litres), including the starter. Make up the remaining 1 lb (450 g) sugar into 1 pint (570 ml) SSS. Ferment on pulp for three to four days in order to obtain a really rich colour. Pass must through a filter bag, expressing as much juice as possible from the pulp. Use a press if available but take care not to crush the stones. Continue fermentation under an airlock. Make SSS additions as required and water if necessary, to finish at 1 gallon (5 litres). Campden, rack and fine as necessary, finally sweetening to 1.020 or to taste.

(11) Damson: Style, Red Table (Approx 12% Alc)

> 3 lb (1.5 kg) fully ripened damsons
> 8 oz (225 g) sultanas
> 1 lb 12 oz (800 g) sugar
> $\frac{1}{4}$ oz (7 g) citric acid
> Pectolytic enzyme
> Yeast nutrient
> 1 × 3 mg vitamin B$_1$ tablet
> 1 campden tablet (or measured stock solution)
> Burgundy, Bordeaux or general-purpose yeast starter

Method
Generally as outlined above for the dessert style, but finally sweetening only to 1.000 or thereabouts for table use.

ELDERBERRY

Elderberries can make a really splendid wine and they come absolutely free. Dried elderberries are also available for winemaking, and whilst these may satisfy a need for all year round use it would be pointless to use them in season when fresh fruit is available. (See also comments about elderberries under Blackberry Table Dry.) It may be recalled that in Chapter Seven it was demonstrated how smaller vessels had an increasingly greater surface area in relation to their volume. Clearly, this is also true of the fruits we use and because elderberries are so small it follows that a given weight will have a total surface area far greater than an equivalent weight of damsons. And because tannin is contained in the skin of the fruit it also follows that elderberries are likely to contain an excessive amount of tannin. Therefore, if a really good wine is to be produced this factor must always be observed. Whilst the fruit must be fully ripe, it should not be gathered late otherwise the tannin content will have increased and flavour will have been adversely affected. In a 'bad' year this problem can be heightened.

So we must not use too much of the fruit and we should not ferment on the pulp for very long. In fact, with elderberries many winemakers resort to what is called a 'second mashing', so as to make both a dessert and table style using the same fruit. This method of working is very successful and convenient and is therefore described here. For those wishing to make only a table wine a separate recipe is also included.

(12) Elderberry: Style, Red Dessert (Approx 16% Alc)

> 4 lb (1.8 kg) fully ripened elderberries
> 1 lb (450 g) sultanas
> 2 lb (900 g) over-ripe bananas
> $2\frac{1}{4}$ lb (1.1 kg) sugar
> $\frac{1}{2}$ oz (14 g) citric acid
> Pectolytic enzyme
> Tronozymol
> 1 campden tablet (or measured stock solution)
> Port, Burgundy or similar yeast starter

Method

Prepare yeast starter. Prepare fruits and add to sterilized bucket as previously described. Deal with elderberries as outlined in recipe six. Prepare a banana gravy (see recipe eight) and when cooled add to the bucket. Mix in pectolytic enzyme, fit bucket lid and place aside for 24 hours. Dissolve $1\frac{1}{4}$ lb (565 g) sugar in a little warmed water and add this, together with all remaining ingredients, making the quantity up to 7 pints (4 litres) with warmed water to finish at 75°F (24°C) including the active starter. Make up the remaining 1 lb (450 g) sugar as SSS. Ferment on pulp for two-and-a-half to three days — no longer. Strain off pulp through a filter bag; press lightly by hand. Transfer this pulp back to the original bucket, fitting the lid immediately (see below). Continue fermentation of the dessert under an airlock, making SSS and water additions if necessary, to finish at 1 gallon (5 litres). Campden, rack and fine in due course as necessary, finally sweetening to taste.

Immediately following hand pressing, transfer attention to the retained pulp to make a table wine.

(12a) Elderberry: Style, Red Table (Approx 12% Alc)

> Pulp from previous dessert fermentation
> 8 oz (225 g) sultanas
> 2 lb (900 g) sugar
> $\frac{3}{4}$ oz (22 g) citric acid (or acid mixture)
> Yeast nutrient
> 1 campden tablet (or measured stock solution)

Method

Note that a yeast starter is not necessary here as all the yeast needed is already in the retained pulp. Add all the remaining ingredients, prepared as previously described, retaining 1 lb (450 g) of the sugar to be added later as SSS and make up to 7 gallons (4 litres) to finish at 75°F (24°C). Ferment on pulp for three to four days, no longer, strain and press in the usual way and ferment to dryness, finishing at 1 gallon (5 litres). Campden, rack and fine as necessary, finally sweetening, if required, to 1.005 or thereabouts.

(13) Elderberry: Style, Red Table (Approx 12% Alc)

$2\frac{1}{2}$ lb (1.13 kg) fully ripened elderberries
8 oz (225 g) sultanas
2 lb (900 g) sugar
$\frac{3}{8}$ oz (11 g) tartaric or acid mixture
Pectolytic enzyme
Yeast nutrient
1 × 3 mg vitamin B_1 tablet
Burgundy, Bordeaux or general-purpose yeast starter
1 campden tablet (or measured stock solution)

Method
Prepare initially as for elderberry dessert, excluding banana gravy, and place aside for 24 hours. Dissolve 1 lb (450 g) sugar in a little warmed water and add, together with all remaining ingredients, extending the quantity to 7 pints (4 litres), including the active starter, to finish at 75°F (24°C). Ferment on pulp for two-and-a-half to three days, no longer; strain off pulp and press lightly. Continue fermentation under an airlock, adding SSS made with the remaining 1 lb (450 g) sugar, adding water if necessary to finish at 1 gallon (5 litres). Campden, rack and fine as necessary, ultimately sweetening to 1.005.

GOOSEBERRY

The value of gooseberries in winemaking has long been acknowledged, and with a little care a very good hock style can be made. However, they have a rather strong aroma which is not appreciated by all and, of course, this particularly affects the dessert variety due to their high fruit content. Accordingly, a recipe for a dessert style is not included here. But I appreciate many may not agree and in such cases one can very readily produce one's own dessert style having studied Chapter Fourteen.

It is better to use a mixture of both cooking and dessert varieties if possible, with the dessert variety predominating. A useful alternative is to use canned gooseberries and in the following recipe the fresh gooseberries may be substituted by 3 × 1 lb 3 oz (540 g) cans per gallon (5 litres). If this course is followed the sugar may be reduced to $1\frac{1}{4}$ lb (565 g) and $\frac{1}{30}$ oz (1 g) of grape tannin should also be added to the must.

(14) Gooseberry: Style, White Table (Approx 12% Alc)

$2\frac{1}{2}$ lb (1.13 kg) mixed ripe gooseberries
1 lb (450 g) sultanas
$1\frac{3}{4}$ lb (800 g) sugar
Pectolytic enzyme
Yeast nutrient
1 × 3 mg vitamin B_1 tablet
1 campden tablet (or measured stock solution)
Hock or general-purpose yeast

Method

Make up yeast starter. Prepare fruits and add to sterilized bucket as previously described. Deal with fresh gooseberries by crushing thoroughly in the bucket. There is no need to top and tail them. Add minced sultanas and extra water if necessary, to keep fruit covered. Mix in the pectolytic enzyme, fit bucket lid and place aside for 24 hours. Make up must to 7 pints (4 litres) as previously described, mixing in all the remaining ingredients and 12 oz (340 g) sugar. Ferment on pulp for five to six days, strain and continue fermentation to completion under an airlock. Campden, rack and fine as necessary and sweeten very slightly if necessary.

LOGANBERRY

Loganberries are rather an exotic fruit, quite expensive to buy and not always easy to locate, but a truly fine wine can be made from them. Their extremely pleasant flavour, high in acid, is unmistakable and this, combined with their relatively high cost, renders them better for a dessert rather than a table style. I personally like this wine and make it at any season of the year from canned fruit. Such a recipe is given below. No acid addition is included as there is usually sufficient in the fruit, but a little extra may be added later to taste if this is thought to be necessary. As the fruit contains mainly citric acid, either tartaric and/or malic additions should be considered, especially with regard to maturing.

133

(15) Loganberry: Style, Red Dessert (Approx 16% Alc)

3 × 14½ oz (410 g) cans Cape loganberries in syrup
½ pint (285 ml) red grape concentrate
2 lb (900 g) sugar
Pectolytic enzyme
Tronozymol
1 campden tablet (or measured stock solution)
Burgundy or general-purpose yeast starter

Method

Prepare yeast starter. Empty contents of cans and measured grape concentrate into a sterile bucket containing 1 pint (570 ml) water into which a campden tablet has been dissolved. Stir in the pectolytic enzyme, fit bucket lid and place aside for 24 hours. Dissolve 1 lb (450 g) sugar in a little warmed water and add this, together with remaining ingredients, diluting with warmed water to finish at 7 pints (4 litres) and at 75°F (24°C) including the active starter. Ferment on pulp for four to five days. Strain and press through filter bag. Continue fermentation under an airlock, making SSS additions and a little water if necessary, to finish at 1 gallon (5 litres). Campden, rack and fine as necessary. Adjust sugar and acid, to taste.

ORANGE

Oranges are another really fine medium and being one of our most popular fruits, there are no drawbacks regarding price or availability. In fact the cheapest and simplest form to use as the base ingredient is ready-prepared, unsweetened orange juice as served at breakfast and available from any supermarket. Messing about with oranges, other than say Seville marmalade oranges, is a waste of time. Both table and dessert styles are popular but the very distinctive flavour of oranges renders them most suitable to the heavier bodied dessert and aperitif styles. The main acid is citric, which renders the must highly fermentable, so any acid additions should be those providing a maturing enhancement. The following recipe makes a really fine wine which can be thoroughly recommended. I regularly make 5 or 10 gallons (23 or 46 litres) each year in the dessert style. It can be drunk and appreciated whilst quite young, but benefits greatly from lengthy maturing. The recipe lends itself to sugar feeding (which is dealt with in Chapter Fourteen).

(16) Orange: Style, White Medium Aperitif or Dessert (Approx 16% Alc)

> 1 quart (1.22 litres) can pure unsweetened orange juice
> 5 medium size Seville oranges
> 1 lb (450 g) sultanas
> 2 $\frac{1}{4}$ lb (1 kg) sugar
> $\frac{1}{8}$ oz (4 g) each tartaric and malic acid
> Pectolytic enzyme
> Tronozymol
> 1 campden tablet (or measured stock solution)
> Sherry, Sauternes or similar yeast starter

Method

Prepare yeast starter. Transfer orange juice to a sterilized bucket containing 1 pint (570 ml) water into which a campden tablet has been dissolved. Mince the sultanas and add to the juice. Peel the outer skins of Seville oranges very thinly using a sharp potato peeler (rather like peeling an apple), so that the peel is bright orange on *both* sides, and add to the must. Halve the oranges and squeeze the juice and body from the white peel using a lemon squeezer. Stir in the pectolytic enzyme, fit bucket lid and place aside for 24 hours. Dissolve 1$\frac{1}{4}$ lb (565 g) sugar in a little warmed water and add this to the must, together with the remaining ingredients and water to finish at 7 pints (4 litres) and 75°F (24°C) including the active starter. Make up the remaining 1 lb (450 g) sugar as SSS. Ferment on the pulp for four to five days. Pass through a filter bag to remove pulp and peel, and continue fermentation under an airlock, making SSS additions and water if necessary, to finish at 1 gallon (5 litres). Rack, fine and sweeten as necessary. For an aperitif style, sweeten to 1.010–1.015 and for a dessert style to 1.030 or to taste.

Note:

On no account must the white pith or pips be allowed into the must otherwise the wine will taste quite bitter and unpalatable.

(17) Orange: Style, White Dessert (Approx 16% Alc)

1 quart (1.22 litres) can pure unsweetened orange juice
$\frac{1}{2}$ pint (285 ml) white grape concentrate
2 lb (900 g) peeled, over-ripe bananas
2 lb (900 g) sugar
$\frac{1}{8}$ oz (4 g) malic acid or acid mix
Pectolytic enzyme
Tronozymol
1 campden tablet (or measured stock solution)
Sherry, Sauternes or similar yeast starter

Method

Prepare yeast starter. Transfer orange juice and grape concentrate to a sterilized bucket containing 1 pint (570 ml) water to which a campden tablet has been added. Peel and slice the bananas and prepare a banana gravy, discarding the pulp as previously described. Allow to cool; add to bucket. Stir in pectolytic enzyme. Fit bucket lid and place aside for 24 hours. Dissolve 1 lb (450 g) sugar in a little warmed water and add to the must, together with the remaining ingredients and water to finish at 7 pints (4 litres) and 75°F (24°C) including the active starter. Add the remaining 1 lb (450 g) sugar as SSS as required. Note this is a juice fermentation and the whole can take place under an airlock as soon as fermentation has subsided sufficiently. Rack, fine and sweeten to taste.

PLUM

(18) Plum: Style, Red, Rosé and White Dessert (Approx 16% Alc)

Plums make an excellent dessert wine which may be made in precisely the same way as described for damson. However, even if a very dark variety is used the resultant wine will not be really red unless some other substantially coloured fruit is used in combination, such as elderberries or blackberries. The acid level is also likely to be somewhat lower so, in using the damson recipe, make a citric acid addition of $\frac{1}{4}$ oz (7 g). Tzar is a really good variety for winemaking.

Plum stones are often somewhat easier to remove than those of damsons, so that plums may merely be cut in half for this purpose before adding to the fermentation bucket. However, if the stones are stubborn treat as recommended for damsons. This wine matures to an excellent port style and the lesser coloured 'dark' varieties tend to brown somewhat, when the wine acquires tawny port characteristics. For this reason it is well worth treating both damson and plum wines to sugar feeding technique, described in the following chapter, in an effort to boost the alcohol content nearer to that of commercially produced port. Or it can be reinforced with spirit, as described in Chapter Nine, but, of course, this is more expensive.

The above comments apply to the black and red varieties. In the same way, yellow and green varieties — the gages — may be used to produce good, white desserts but any secondary fruit additions must also be white.

RASPBERRY

(19) Raspberry: Style, Rosé Dessert (Approx 16% Alc)

Although somewhat more abundant than loganberries, raspberries are in the same category in that, in the fresh form, they are rather too expensive for quantity winemaking. In fact, because such good wines can be made from far less exotic fruits, my wife always insists that any fresh raspberries we may acquire be reserved in the freezer for future flan making! She has learnt by experience, so who am I to argue! The supermarket is not far away and a very good wine can be made from the canned variety with the added advantage of year-round availability. The recipe given for loganberries may therefore also be used here, substituting the same quantity of raspberries. In this case, however, a delightful rosé is produced having a very pleasant and unmistakable flavour. The acid level may be somewhat lower than for loganberries, so $\frac{1}{8}$ oz (4 g) will need to be added, and as the acid in raspberries is essentially citric, the addition should be either tartaric or malic, or even a little of both, especially if you intend to allow it to mature.

STRAWBERRY

Strawberry wine has a most unmistakable flavour, well appreciated in the right circumstances, and is best suited to a good dessert style. Strawberries are very plentiful and not particularly expensive in season, especially if you intend to 'pick-your-own', and so a recipe is given using fresh fruits.

(20) Strawberry: Style, Rosé Dessert (Approx 16% Alc)

> 3 lb (1.5 kg) fresh strawberries
> 12 oz (340 g) sultanas
> $2\frac{1}{2}$ lb (1.13 kg) sugar
> $\frac{1}{30}$ oz (1 g) grape tannin
> $\frac{1}{4}$ oz (7 g) tartaric, malic or mixed acid
> Pectolytic enzyme
> Tronozymol
> 1 campden tablet (or measured stock solution)
> Tokay or Port yeast starter

Method

Prepare yeast starter. Wash strawberries, removing stalks, and crush in a sterile bucket containing 1 pint (570 ml) water into which a campden tablet has been dissolved. Mince sultanas and add to bucket. Increase amount of water if necessary to keep fruit just covered. Mix in the pectolytic enzyme, fit bucket lid and place aside for 24 hours. Dissolve $1\frac{1}{2}$ lb (680 g) sugar in a little warmed water and add to must, together with remaining ingredients, finally making up the volume to 7 pints (4 litres) including the active starter. Make up the remaining 1 lb (450 g) sugar into SSS. Ferment on pulp for four to five days. Pass through a filter bag, expressing juice into must and continue fermentation under an airlock. Make SSS and water additions as required to finish at 1 gallon (5 litres). Campden, rack and fine as necessary, finally sweetening to 1.020 or to taste.

CHAPTER 14

DEVISING YOUR OWN RECIPES

The foregoing recipes are very useful for those not wishing to produce their own or who may simply not have the time available to do more than follow a minimum of instructions. Certainly, good wine can be produced from working to any one of them. However, it is always better to understand a recipe so that it can be adjusted to suit the ingredients available at that time. Once this ability is acquired it becomes second nature until there should be no problem whatsoever in producing good wines from any fruits at hand, even though a recipe may not be available. Indeed the best wines are made in this way and, as explained in the foreword, it is for this reason that a proliferation of recipes has been deliberately avoided. It is the 'rational' approach.

Winemaking Fruits

Appendix VI is a comprehensive list showing the general characteristics of popular fruits. It may look formidable but it is not. It is supplied merely as a reference and includes most of the fruits one is likely to find available. Much has already been said about the eminent suitability of grapes for winemaking and how first class wines can often be produced from these with no additions whatsoever. Everything required for a good fermentation is intrinsic in the fruit and, in the most favourable conditions, even water is unnecessary though in excess of 10 lb (4.5 kg) grapes per gallon (5 litres) may be required. Indeed, a glance at the chart shows grapes as being 'medium in all things' except sugar, which is conveniently high in readiness for transformation into alcohol. It is also clear from the chart that no other fruit is nearly so well endowed and, indeed,

139

most of the fruits available to us, other than dried fruits, are extremely low in sugar. They all show excesses or deficiencies in some way or other and so it becomes necessary to make certain adjustments if a good wine is to be produced from them.

Generally speaking, it has been found that 6 lb (2.72 kg) fruit per gallon (5 litres) will be required for a dessert style wine, whilst about 50 to 60% of this quantity is required for the table style. The latter are, of course, of lower alcohol content to enable us to take a longer drink with meals and are also of less flavour so as not to detract from enjoyment of the food. These factors give us a starting point. Let us consider the recipe in Chapter Thirteen: (13) Elderberries: Style, Red Table (Approx 12% Alc). From the above recommended quantities it will be clear that some 3 to $3\frac{1}{2}$ lb (1.5 to 1.58 kg) per gallon (5 litres) may be required, but from columns one, two and four, flavour, body and tannin respectively, we can deduce that perhaps it would be better to lower these values somewhat for a table wine because both flavour and tannin are high; so it appears that $2\frac{1}{2}$ lb (1.13 kg) per gallon (5 litres) would be about right. This will bring down the remaining values in proportion but it is always easier to make additions rather than subtractions. Even so, elderberries are so high in tannin that it is invariably recommended that pulp fermentation be very limited before they are removed from the must and the remaining juice expressed.

Body

Next we must consider what is referred to as the 'body additions', and in this category there is considerable choice. Grape concentrate, sultanas, raisins, figs, dates, prunes and bananas added in moderation increase body (and sugar) without adversely affecting the chosen fruit flavour. But in the example currently being considered it would be foolish to add too much body. Nevertheless, three of these, namely grape concentrate, sultanas and raisins, are always good additions to make — even if only a small amount is added — because they are all based on grapes and therefore provide many of the trace elements necessary for a good fermentation. It is good to get into the habit of adding a little of one or other of these three to all our musts and, perhaps in the case of dessert wines, in combination with one or a number of the remainder. There is no strict rule about which to add. In the case of a juice fermentation grape concentrate is clearly best because it adds no pulp to be removed later, but with pulp fermentation either sultanas or raisins will suffice and are somewhat cheaper. I use sultanas for pulp fermentation since they are cheaper than raisins and, being based on white grapes, may be added to either white or red varieties. The same can be said of grape concentrate. White concentrate may be added to either white or red wines, and indeed red concentrate may be added to a white must as a way of creating a rosé if required. But if one requires to increase the red wine character of a wine made from red fruits then the use of a red concentrate is clearly better. Normally, $\frac{1}{4}$ pint (140 ml) to 1 pint (570 ml) grape concentrate per gallon (5 litres) should be used, or 8 oz–1 lb (225–450 g) of sultanas or raisins. Because the example under consideration is a table style, involving a pulp fermentation with plenty of colour and tannin, the mid point, $\frac{1}{2}$ pint (285 ml) or 8 oz (225 g) of the additives is employed.

Having prepared these two ingredients as described earlier and subjecting them to a campden solution, it is merely required to add pectolytic enzyme before placing aside for 24 hours. Some authors recommend an upper and lower quantity of pectolytic enzyme to be added for the various wine styles — generally more for the dessert style due to the higher quantity of fruit. Column three indicates that pectin in elderberries is medium and therefore a medium dosage for the table style will be about right.

A word about additions here, not only pectolytic enzyme, but also all other additives. It must be borne in mind that yeast is a living organism, and like all organisms needs to be fed. However, in the case of plants, we eat the products of the kitchen garden, not the soil in which they are grown; in the case of our wines, we ultimately dispose of the plants and consume their environment! This is rather akin to consuming earth and any residual plant nutrient we may have added! Clearly this is an analogy but it serves to illustrate the point that, whilst we must use sufficient nutrients or other additives to provide the result we want, we should not be over-generous for any remaining materials of this sort would certainly not improve flavour of the finished product and indeed may have deleterious effects, often bestowing a salty taste upon the wine!

Tannin

After the elapse of 24–48 hours during which time the starter will have become active, the stage is reached where the remaining ingredients are to be added. The next item convenient for consideration is tannin. This is very difficult for the amateur to assess but, happily, though it is the compound which provides part of the necessary astringency to a wine, especially a red wine, its measured quantity is not absolutely critical. Suffice it to say that white wine contains rather less than red and the heavier bodied wines should contain more than the lighter. So, for the amateur, tannin additions must be a matter for judgement, in which it is hoped column four of the chart will be of some assistance. Of course pulp fermentations produce more tannin than juice fermentations because tannin is obtained from the skin of the fruit, as is colour. But we must not be fooled by this, for quite a number of the fruits producing white wines contain a large amount of tannin — as will be seen from the chart.

Acid

The quantity of acid required must be considered. The chart indicates that the predominant acid in elderberries is citric, but there is not likely to be very much of it. And in this case the sum total will be low since we have deliberately kept the fruit level down due to its strong flavour and high tannin content.

The way to measure the acid content in parts per thousand (ppt) of a juice and relate this to the finished quantity is outlined in Chapter Twelve. Having calculated any deficiency, Appendix III is a convenient table indicating quantities of the various acids which may be added. However, the case under consideration is pulp fermentation and so the acid cannot be very easily measured by titration, as any liquid taken from the must before fermentation will not include the bulk of the acid which is still in the fruit. It therefore becomes necessary to refer to average acid content in the fruit as shown below. This is quite satisfactory at this stage, especially to ensure that there is sufficient acid for a good fermentation. During fermentation, the acidity will increase by about one ppt, although I prefer to ignore this and regard it as the amount which will subsequently be lost during maturation. In short, with both juice and pulp fermentations it is as well to check acidity after fermentation is complete, and adjust if necessary as soon as it is certain that all residual carbon dioxide (CO_2) remaining in the bulk has dispersed. When finally testing, do not worry if the acid level is somewhat higher than recommended — maturation will tend to take care of this. But always increase the acid if it is low. There is nothing worse than a dull, insipid wine, even though its alcohol content may be high.

Example: (Assessing Acid in a Pulp Must)
One gallon (5 litres) of water weighs 10 lb (4.5 kg) and so, because the specific gravity of a finished wine is about 1.000, it follows that 1 gallon (5 litres) of wine also weighs about 10 lb (4.5 kg). Neglecting

that a little pulp debris is finally removed, each pound (450 g) of fruit may be considered to contribute 10% of the finished gallon. The chart indicates that elderberries contain an average of 10 ppt acid in the flesh, and hence 10 ppt acid in each pound of fruit must represent one ppt in the gallon (5 litres). And, as $2\frac{1}{2}$ lb (1.13 kg) elderberries are used, then the overall acidity becomes $1 \times 2\frac{1}{2} = 2.5$ ppt. From Appendix I, a dry red table wine should have an acidity of 4 ppt. Therefore the must has a deficiency of $4 - 2.5 = 1.5$ ppt. And, from Appendix III, 1.5 ppt deficiency calls for 10.5 g tartaric acid which is approximately $\frac{3}{8}$ oz. Remember that this is only an approximation at this stage and that a final, more accurate assessment can be made by titration of the finished wine. One of the other acids may be used instead because citric acid, though very acceptable for taste, is already present in the fruit and it is of little use for maturing. Malic acid could well be used as tartaric acid is present in the sultanas anyway.

Sugar

Only sugar remains to be considered, and this is simplest of all. From Appendix V Gravity Tables — or reading directly from your saccharometer — it will be seen that a finished wine of 12% alcohol requires an initial overall specific gravity in the order of 1.090, which represents approximately 38 oz (1 kg) sugar. Now the total sugar in this recipe must be that contained in the elderberries *plus* that in the sultanas *plus* the sugar added, as under:

$2\frac{1}{2}$ lb (1.1 kg) elderberries
at 8% sugar   = 3 oz (80 g)
                                     approx
8 oz (225 g) sultanas at 50 % sugar = 4 oz (110 g)
                                       approx
Sugar addition   = x

                   Total   = 38 oz (1.1 kg)
∴ Amount sugar required to be added = $38 - 7 = 31$ oz
                                     (900 g)

That is approximately <u>2 lb</u> (1 kg)

Dessert Wines

The dessert style is dealt with in exactly the same way as the table wine but the greater fruit quantity and higher alcohol content will modify the figures somewhat. It now only remains to consider a juice fermentation and to say something additional about the dessert style, so let us consider the recipe (17) Orange: Style, White Dessert (Approx 16% Alc).

In this example, Appendix VI indicates that flavour, tannin and acid are likely to be plentiful, but that for a dessert style a little extra body would be beneficial without appreciably increasing or modifying flavour. Hence a banana gravy is advocated in addition to the grape concentrate. This is prepared as described in the method relating to the recipe.

Firstly, all the fruit ingredients, including the banana gravy, were added to the sterile bucket containing 1 pint (570 ml) water according to the recipe and thoroughly stirred together. Because this is a juice fermentation the overall acid level can be checked by titration easily. In the example, the initial acidity of the orange juice, grape concentrate, banana gravy and 1 pint (570 ml) water = 5.5 ppt and the total volume was 5 pints (2.5 litres). Hence the final calculated acidity, when subsequently extended to make 1 gallon (5 litres) is as follows:

$$\frac{5.5 \times 5}{8} = 3.44 \text{ ppt}$$

But the recommended acidity in Appendix I for a white dessert is 4 to 6 ppt. Hence there is a deficiency of at least 0.56 ppt which needs to be made up. It will be seen that the ingredients provide citric, tartaric and malic acid and so the type of acid to be added is not really critical, but malic was chosen as it is a good maturer. Appendix III shows that 0.5 ppt deficiency requires $3\frac{1}{4}$ g malic acid, and so $\frac{1}{8}$ oz (4 g) was adopted as a practical addition.

Having decided upon the ingredients and their quantity, and assessed and adjusted the acid, it merely remained to assess the sugar content in the fruit so that the remaining sugar requirement may be calculated. A saccharometer reading of a sample taken from the 5 pints indicated that the specific gravity was 1.063, which corresponds to a sugar content of approximately $26\frac{1}{2}$ oz per gallon (5 litres). This can be seen from Appendix V, or it may be read directly from the saccharometer. But only 5 pints (2.85 litres) of liquid was tested so the sugar content per gallon (5 litres), when made up with water, would be as follows:

$$\frac{26.5 \times 5}{8} = 16.56 \text{ oz}$$

Again from Appendix V (or from the saccharometer), the total sugar requirement for a final 16% V/V alcohol content is marginally over 49 oz. Therefore additional sugar required = 49–16.56 = 32.44 oz, say 2 lb (1 kg).

It will be appreciated from the above example that all values are measured and no average figures have been used as must be the case with pulp musts. Thus it will be clear that in pulp fermentation of the dessert style, where fermentation is pushed to the limit, there is a possibility of having a little too much sugar available on occasions and that the specific gravity of the finished wine will indicate a residue of unfermented sugar. However, provided the must was well balanced and that it was fermented in one of the ways advocated in Chapter Seven, the residue will not present a problem. For example, assume that your wine finished with a specific gravity of 1.007; Appendix V indicates that the residual sugar is approximately 3 oz (80 g) per gallon (5 litres). It will be seen that in sweetening to 1.025, 10 oz (280 g) sugar would normally be needed. Therefore in this particular example, only 7 oz (200 g) per gallon (5 litres) would be needed for sweetening.

Now a point regarding the dessert wines referred to in Chapter Thirteen. Many would say that these really come into the category of social wines and which, generally speaking, fall midway between the normally accepted table and dessert styles so far as fruit and alcohol content are concerned. The fruit and alcohol level of these recipes are at the upper limit for the social style which, in my view, brings them into the dessert category. Nevertheless, the alcoholic strength of any one of these recipes may be increased by fortification, which is dealt with under that sub-heading in Chapter Nine. Most home winemakers rarely resort to fortification because of the considerable expense involved. It tends to be regarded as some sort of concession to defeat, and one of the main objectives of home winemaking is to avoid the heavy rate of duty levied against such products.

In order to achieve roughly a similar result, and with much more satisfaction, many of the more experienced resort to what is termed 'sugar feeding', which again sounds far more formidable than is actually the case. By now it will be understood how yeast gradually expends itself by using up the sugar on which it thrives and progressively polluting its own environment with alcohol in so doing. Normally this point is reached at about 16% V/V, as in the case of the foregoing dessert recipes. Nevertheless, this is almost the strength of a good commercial port or sherry and would certainly be accepted as being an ideal home dessert. But to get these levels of alcohol the methods of must preparation, fermentation and temper-ature maintenance advocated in this book should be observed in all respects. They are certainly not for those who prefer fermentation at 60°F (16°C). And, of course, a good robust yeast such as Port, Sherry or Madeira is necessary too.

The object of making-up our 1 gallon (5 litres) musts to 7 pints (4 litres) initially by leaving out 1 pint (570 ml) of strong sugar syrup enables us to use it for 'feeding' the must progressively following the initial vigorous fermentation. This trains the yeast to get used to a steady diet which helps to ensure that fermentation is carried through to completion.

In this way it is sometimes possible to gain a somewhat higher alcohol content by feeding-in rather more than the one pint of syrup. To do this you will need to leave out a little more water from the must initially and have to hand an equivalent amount of extra syrup. But don't expect to feed in more than an extra few ounces.

Here is how it is done. Following vigorous fermentation, check the specific gravity. When it falls to 1.010, or thereabouts, add $\frac{1}{4}$ pint (140 ml) of syrup. Make a further addition when the specific gravity falls to 1.005 and thereafter continue to make $\frac{1}{8}$ pint (70 ml) addition each time the specific gravity falls to one.

When activity becomes very slow and there is very little gravity change over a few days, add no more syrup but remember that, as there is a remainder you will have less than a finished 8 pints (4.7 litres) of wine. So, if it appears sugar will be left over, add a very small amount of water alongside the last couple of syrup additions. This will lower the alcohol concentration somewhat and, hopefully, enable a little further fermentation to take place. Remember that the aim is for maximum alcohol in the full gallon (5 litres) and clearly this cannot be achieved if topping-up with water is necessary after fermentation ceases.

By keeping a note of the total sugar converted to alcohol it will be possible to assess the alcohol content.

In conclusion, remember that the figures of 6 lb (2.72 kg) fruit per gallon (5 litres) of dessert, and approximately 50 to 60% for the table style is purely arbitrary, and a glance at Appendix VI will indicate that some judgement will be needed in many cases. There are one or two very considerable exceptions, and perhaps blackcurrants best illustrate this point. It will be seen from the table that the specified minimum acidity in the fruit is 55 ppt. Clearly if we were to use 6 lb (2.72 kg) of fruit in the 10 lb (4.5 kg) (1-gallon or 5-litre) batch the acidity is likely to be:

$$\frac{55 \times 6}{10} = 33 \text{ ppt}$$

As a dessert style red requires an acidity of approximately 6.0 ppt, this is much too high. To provide the correct acidity, the amount of fruit (x) would need to be

$$x = \frac{6.0 \times 10}{55} = 1.1 \text{ lb (475 g) or about 17 oz}$$

Clearly, this quantity would not provide sufficient body or tannin, especially for a dessert style and it is highly likely that flavour too, would be unsatisfactory. Hence, in recipe (8) — Blackcurrant: Style, Rosé Dessert, in addition to the 1 lb (450 g) blackcurrants advocated, it is backed up with a generous measure of grape juice and additionally a banana gravy. In order to identify the blackcurrant flavour, some winemakers increase the calculated quantity and mask the extra acid with additional sweetening, but it is certainly difficult to reconcile the high volume of blackcurrants advocated in some books.

FINAL THOUGHTS

In conclusion, it is hoped that sufficient has been said to stimulate your enthusiasm and confidence in devising your own wine recipes whenever sufficient and suitable fruits are to hand, and that the tables, particularly Appendices V and VI, will be of assistance. But don't forget to add the nutrients, energisers and clearing agents as may be required. Without a printed recipe it is very easy to overlook certain items so it is a good idea to get used to writing down the recipe first. In this way you will also have a useful future reference without having to commit anything to memory.

The theme of this book is based on success rather than rescue, so that hopefully you will have little need of the following and last chapter dealing with faults and remedies. I will therefore, take this opportunity of wishing you every success.

CHAPTER 15

FAULTS AND REMEDIES

Sadly, no winemaking book would be complete without some emphasis on the problems one may encounter. These fall into two general categories, namely chemical and micro-biological. Fortunately most faults are of the former.

The more common faults together with their remedies are given in the table below.

CHEMICAL FAULTS

FAULT	SYMPTOMS AND REMEDY
1/. STUCK FERMENTATIONS May be due to any	
a) **Incorrect Temperature**.	The most common fault. Use a recognized method of temperature control. If stuck at a late stage, doubling-up procedure may be necessary.
b) **Excess Sugar**.	Dilute with water, or mix with a dry wine should the over-sweet wine be of a light nature and unable to take dilution. This may also call for re-adjustment of acid level to suit the resulting wine style.
c) **Acid Imbalance**.	Usually a deficiency. Check and adjust as necessary.
d) **Under-developed Yeast Colony**.	If little or no fermentation has occurred, aerate vigorously. Add new vigorously fermented yeast

starter. For further advanced fermentation, doubling-up may be necessary.

e) **High Level of Sulphiting at the initial stage — detect presence of excess by smell.**

Aerate must for a few days to reduce level of sulphite and proceed as outlined in d) above.

f) **Nutrient Deficiency.**

Ensure added as per recipe or maker's instructions.

2/. HAZES

a) Pectin Haze.

Test for pectin by applying methylated spirit test. Add pectolytic enzyme at any stage — although it will be less efficient in the presence of the alcohol that has formed.

b) Starch Haze.

Mainly in vegetables but also in some fruit. Apply starch test (see page 86). Treat with amylase: as for pectolytic enzyme above.

c) Protein Haze.

Use a wine fining gel or Bentonite.

d) Metallic Haze.

Caused by use of incorrect equipment. No cure. Dispose of wine. Do not drink — poisonous.

3/. UNPLEASANT FLAVOURS

a) Oxidation.

Occurs during prolonged, unsatisfactory storage. Too much contact with air, especially at higher storage temperatures which accelerate

CHEMICAL FAULTS

FAULT	SYMPTOMS AND REMEDY
	the condition. Whether white or red wine, the colour browns and acquires a sherry-like odour. No cure. Discard if the taste is unacceptable.
b) **Maturing on Lees**	Musty smell and taste. Rack all wines regularly, especially following fermentation. There is no cure; discard.
c) **Acid Excess**	Any of the following approaches may be used. 1. Blend with a low acid wine. 2. Dilute with water. 3. Use acid reducing agent. 4. Mask with extra sugar. 5. Mature for lengthy period. 6. Reduce tartaric acid by refrigerating and decanting.
d) **Acid Deficiency**	a) Medicinal taste. Discard if pronounced. Unsuitable for blending. b) Blend with a wine of high acid. c) Make acid addition.
e) **Tannin Excess**	Unpleasantly astringent. Blend with a tannin-deficient wine. Mature for lengthy period. Increasing sweetness will mask slight excesses of tannin.
f) **Tannin Deficiency**	Make small additions of proprietary tannin to taste — preferably liquid variety at this stage.

MICRO-BIOLOGICAL FAULTS

a) Acetification

Acetic acid is the compound that gives vinegar its characteristic taste and an acetified wine has a similar flavour and smell. It is caused by a bacteria known as *Acetobacter* which oxidizes the alcohol to acetic acid.

Early detection during fermentation may save the wine if treated with two crushed campden and the fermentation re-started a day or so later by the 'doubling-up' process.

The micro-organism causing acetification may be introduced into the must in a number of ways, including the small fruit flies frequently seen hovering around decaying fruits and any exposed fruit juices. Fermentation buckets should always have their lids pressed firmly down not only to prevent the entry of the flies, but to ensure that there is only a minimum quantity of air in contact with the wine. Oxygen is necessary for the conversion of alcohol into acetic acid. Similarly during all stages of maturation the containers should be kept topped up with liquid and corked.

b) Flowers of Wine

Flowers of wine starts as white flecks on the surface of a finished wine and grows until it covers the liquid completely with a white film. It is due to the infection *Candida Mycoderma*. It is similar to acetification as it only occurs in the presence of air and destroys the alcohol, converting it to carbon dioxide and water.

Treatment is as above immediately the first white flecks are seen. Allow deposit to settle and drink early.

c) Ropiness

This is a condition which produces a quite alarming, oily appearance in a finished wine, causing it to pour rather like an oil. It is often accompanied by a slimy rope-like growth. However, both alcohol content and flavour remain unaffected.

Treat with a solution of two campden tablets (or two teaspoons (2 × 5 ml) 10% stock sulphite solution) per gallon (5 litres) of wine, and thoroughly stir the liquid. After two to three days the wine should be racked very carefully. Allow to stabilize for a few weeks but drink at an early date.

d) Tourne Disease

This is caused by a lactic acid bacterial attack. It is easily detected by the silvery sheen that is observed when the container is swirled against a strong light. It is accompanied by a very bitter taste. There is no really satisfactory cure for this malady, even in its early stages, and the wine should be discarded.

e) Malo-lactic Fermentation

This occurs when malic acid is broken-down by a bacteria forming lactic acid which is more mellow to the taste. It occurs in young wines made from fruits containing malic acid — the principal being apples — or wine fermented from musts to which malic acid was added at the preparation stage. It is far less likely to be encountered in sulphited wines.

Occasionally, in a dry wine, one may be fortunate enough to have unintentionally created something very bright and sparkling having Champagne-like characteristics, but if the condition is detected early enough the wine should be put back safely under a fermentation lock as sparkling wines are not the concern of this book and hence no pressure-type glass bottles are advocated.

Malo-lactic fermentation and the consequent mellowing of the wine is considered a bonus by some winemakers, and a fault by others.

APPENDIX I

RECOMMENDED ACIDITY LEVELS

Note: Figures quoted are in parts per thousand (ppt) as sulphuric acid (as measured by titration). Somewhat higher figures are acceptable particularly if long maturation is intended.

Red or White	Dry	4.0
table wines	Medium	4.5
	Sweet	5.0
Rosé		5.0
Dessert	Red	4.0–6.0
(sweet only)	White	4.0–6.0

APPENDIX II

Sulphuric	Citric	Tartaric	Malic
1	1.43	1.53	1.37

Table to convert acidity from sulphuric, as measured by titration, to the three fruit acids.

APPENDIX III

1	2	3	4
PPT	Acid — grams per gallon (5 litres)		
Sulphuric	Citric	Tartaric	Malic
1.0	$6\frac{1}{2}$	7	$6\frac{1}{4}$
2.0	13	14	$12\frac{1}{2}$
3.0	$19\frac{1}{2}$	21	$18\frac{3}{4}$
4.0	26	28	25

Table showing approximate grams weight of acids to be added to 1 gallon (5 litres) of wine to raise acidity relative to sulphuric acid.

APPENDIX IV

Relationship between Proof Spirit° and Alcohol Content V/V

To convert Proof° to Alcohol % V/V
$$\text{Alcohol \% V/V} = \text{Proof}° \times \frac{4}{7}$$

To convert Alcohol % V/V to Proof°
$$\text{Proof}° = \text{Alcohol \%} \times \frac{7}{4}$$

APPENDIX V

GRAVITY TABLES

Specific Gravity	Gravity	Oz Sugar Per Gall	Grams Sugar Per Litre	Potential Alc. % By Volume	Finished Gravity (After) Sweetening	O/A Sugar & Corresponding Start Gravy
0.990						
0.995						
1.000	0	0	0	0	} Dry	
1.005	5	2¼	14	0.6	} Medium	
1.010	10	4	25	1.2	} Dry	
1.015	15	6¼	39	1.9	} Medium	
1.020	20	8¼	51	2.6		
1.025	25	10¼	64	3.3	} Sweet	
1.030	30	13	81	4.0		
1.035	35	15	94	4.7		
1.040	40	17	106	5.3		
1.045	45	19¼	120	6.0	Note: All the sugar is	
1.050	50	21¼	133	6.7	not added initially	
1.055	55	23¾	145	7.4	especially in the higher	
1.060	60	25¼	158	8.2	gravity/alcohol content	
1.065	65	27¼	172	9.0	range (see text).	

1.070	70	$29\frac{1}{2}$	184	9.7	
1.075	75	$31\frac{1}{2}$	197	10.3	
1.080	80	$33\frac{1}{2}$	209	11.0	⎫ 10 – 12% V/V Table Wine
1.085	85	$35\frac{1}{2}$	222	11.6	⎬ (Starting Gravity)
1.090	90	$37\frac{3}{4}$	236	12.3	⎭
1.095	95	40	250	13.0	
1.100	100	$42\frac{1}{2}$	265	13.7	⎫ 12 – 14% V/V Social Wine
1.105	105	$44\frac{1}{2}$	278	14.4	⎬ (Starting Gravity)
1.110	110	$46\frac{1}{2}$	290	15.1	⎭
1.115	115	$48\frac{1}{2}$	303	15.8	⎫ 14 – 16% V/V Dessert Wine
1.120	120	$50\frac{3}{4}$	317	16.6	⎬ (Starting Gravity)
1.125	125	53	331	17.3	⎭
1.130	130	55	343	18.0	Limit to achievable
1.135	135	$57\frac{1}{4}$	357	18.7	alcohol levels
1.140	140	$59\frac{1}{4}$	370	19.5	
1.145	145	$61\frac{1}{2}$	384	20.2	
1.150	150	$63\frac{1}{2}$	396	20.9	
1.155	155	$65\frac{1}{2}$	409	21.6	
1.160	160	$67\frac{3}{4}$	423	22.2	

Note These sugar and potential alcohol figures may not correspond exactly with others published, but alcohol contents are to be taken as a guide only. The figures quoted here are as read directly from a winemaker's saccharometer of reputable make.

APPENDIX VI

CHARACTERISTICS OF POPULAR FRUITS

Fruit	Flavour	Body	Pectin	Tannin
Apple	Low/Med	Low	Med	Low/Med
Apricot (Fresh)	Med	Med	Med	High
Apricot (Dried)	Med	Med	Med	High
• Banana (Fresh)	Med	High	Low	Low
• Banana (Dried)	Med	High	Low	Low
Bilberry (Fresh)	High	Med	Med	High
Bilberry (Dried)	High	Med	Med	High
Blackberry	Med	Med	Med	Med
• Blackcurrant	High	Med	Med	High
Cherry (Sweet)	High	Med	Med	Med
Damson	High	Med	Med	High
• Date (Dried)	High	High	Low	Low
Elderberry	High	Med	Med	V. High
• Figs (Dried)	High	High	Med	High
Gooseberry	Med	Low/Med	High	Low
Grape	Med	Med	Med	Med
Grapefruit	High	Med	High	High
Greengage	Med	Med	Med	Med
• Lemon	High	Med	High	Med
Loganberry	High	Med	High	Med
Orange (Sweet)	High	Med	High	High
Orange (Seville)	High	Med	High	High
Peach	High	Med	Med	High
• Pear	Low	Low	Low	High
• Pineapple	Med	Low	High	Low
Plum	Med	Med	High	High
Prune	High	High	Med	Med
• Raisin	High	High	Med	High
Raspberry	High	Med	High	Med
Strawberry	Med	Low	Med	Low
• Sultana	Med	High	Med	Med

• Fruits marked thus are better used as a secondary ingredient in conjunction with another.

Note: The values are from a number of sources and are given only as a guide to fruit choice, quantity and balance. Tannin (Col. 4) is essentially to be found in fruit skins. This must be taken into account and adjusted, especially for a juice fermentation.

Acid PPT (Sulphuric)		% Weight Sugar in Flesh	
Predominant	Approx Total In Fruit	Min	Max
Malic	2 – 9	8	14
Malic	8 – 15	5	10
Malic	30 – 50	20	35
Citric/Malic	3 – 5	15	21
Citric/Malic	10 – 12	45	60
Citric	8 – 10	9	11
Citric	30 – 40	25	35
Citric/Malic	9 – 13	5	7
Citric	55 – 65	7	10
Malic	4 – 7	7	12
Malic	22 – 25	6	10
	10 – 12	50	70
Citric	6 – 14	7	9
Citric	15 – 25	50	70
Malic	5 – 21	4	8
Tartaric	4 – 12	12	18
Citric	10 – 20	5	7
Malic	9 – 13	7	9
Citric	36 – 40	2	5
Citric	16 – 23	4	8
Citric	9 – 11	6	9
Citric	20 – 35	2	5
Citric/Malic	6 – 9	7	12
Citric	1 – 4	7	14
Citric	8 – 12	8	15
Malic	14 – 18	6	14
Malic	15 – 25	50	70
Tartaric	15 – 40	50	70
Citric	12 – 17	4	8
Citric	9 – 11	5	7
Tartaric	15 – 40	50	70

APPENDIX VII

WEIGHT AND MEASURE COMPARISONS

Note: Values given may be approximate only but are sufficiently accurate for all winemaking purposes.

1. Weight Equivalents

Imperial (oz)	$\frac{1}{30}$	$\frac{1}{15}$	$\frac{1}{6}$	$\frac{1}{4}$	$\frac{1}{3}$	$\frac{3}{4}$	1	4	16 (1 lb)	32 (2 lb)	38
Metric (g)	1	2	5	7	10	22	30	115	450	900	1000 (1 kg)

2. Fluid Equivalents

Imperial		US		Metric
Fl oz	Pint	Fl oz	Pint	(ml)
$\frac{1}{30}$		$\frac{1}{30}$		1
$\frac{1}{4}$		$\frac{1}{4}$		7
$\frac{1}{3}$		$\frac{1}{3}$		10
1		1		30
4		4	$\frac{1}{4}$	120
5	$\frac{1}{4}$	5		140
$8\frac{1}{3}$		$8\frac{3}{4}$	$\frac{1}{2}$	240
10	$\frac{1}{2}$	10		285
17		17	1	475
20	1	20		570
135		135	8 (1 Gall)	3800
160	8 .	160		4500
	(1 Gall)			

APPENDIX VIII

TEMPERATURE CONVERSIONS (to nearest $\frac{1}{2}$ °C)

°Fahrenheit	32	40	50	60	70	80	90	120	150	200	212
°Centigrade	0	$4\frac{1}{2}$	10	$15\frac{1}{2}$	21	$26\frac{1}{2}$	32	49	$65\frac{1}{2}$	$93\frac{1}{2}$	100

INDEX

159